Sea of Galilee
&
Northern Israel Biblical Sites Guide

Sea of Galilee

&

Northern Israel

Biblical Sites Guide

Todd M. Fink

Sea of Galilee
&
Northern Israel

Biblical Sites Guide
by
Todd M. Fink

Published by Selah Book Press

Cover Illustration Copyright © 2021 by Selah Book Press
Cover design by Selah Book Press

Copyright © 2021 by Todd M. Fink

ISBN-13: 978-1-944601-39-3

Second Edition

All rights reserved. No part of this publication may be reproduced or transmitted in any form or by any means, electronic or mechanical, including photocopy, recording, or any information storage retrieval system, without permission in writing from the copyright owner.

Scripture References are taken from the following Bible versions:

New American Standard Bible®,
Copyright © 1960, 1962, 1963, 1968, 1971, 1972, 1973,
1975, 1977, 1995 by The Lockman Foundation
Used by permission. (www.Lockman.org)

The Holy Bible, English Standard Version® (ESV®)
Copyright © 2001 by Crossway,
a publishing ministry of Good News Publishers.
All rights reserved.
ESV Text Edition: 2007

The Holy Bible, New International Version®, NIV® Copyright © 1973, 1978, 1984, 2011 by Biblica, Inc.® Used by permission. All rights reserved worldwide.

The Holy Bible, New King James Version®. Copyright © 1982 by Thomas Nelson, Inc. All rights reserved.

The NET Bible®, New English Translation (NET) Scripture quoted by permission. Quotations designated (NET) are from the NET Bible® copyright ©1996-2006 by Biblical Studies Press, L.L.C.

Scripture in bold is emphasis added by the author.

Table of Contents

Acknowledgments 1
Israel: Land of the Bible 2

Sea of Galilee Sites 4
    Sea of Galilee Overview 5
    Bethsaida 12
    Calling of the Disciples 17
    Capernaum 22
    Chorazin 30
    Feeding the 5,000 35
    Jesus Walks on the Water, Calms the Storm and Sea 40
    Kursi 46
    Magdala: Mary Magdalene 51
    Mount Arbel 56
    Mount of Beatitudes 62
    Sower's Cove: Parables of the Kingdom 67
    Tabgha 72
    Yardenit Baptismal Site 78
    Other Sites Around the Sea of Galilee 80

Northern Israel Sites 85
    Beth-Shean 86
    Beth-Shean Amphitheater/Hippodrome 94
    Caesarea Philippi 102
    Caesarea Maritime 110
    Cana 115
    Dan 119
    Gideon's Spring 125

Hazor	132
Jordan River Overview	138
Megiddo: Valley of Armageddon	144
Mount Carmel	151
Mount Tabor	159
Nazareth Overview	165
Nazareth: Church of the Annunciation	171
Sepphoris (Tsipori, Zippori)	175
Other Sites in Northern Israel	181

Timeline of Israel **185**

Maps of Israel **191**

Twelve Tribes of Israel	192
Divided Kingdom	193
Regions of Israel	194
Israel Today	195

Travel Orientation **196**

Understanding the Holy Sites in Israel	197
How to Get the Most Out of Your Holy Land Trip	200
Understanding Group Travel Dynamics	202
Travel Tips for Israel	204
Packing List	205

About the Author **208**

Books by Todd M. Fink	209
Connect with Todd	210

Acknowledgments

First and foremost, God deserves all the credit and glory for this book. He gave the desire, resources, time, strength, perseverance, and the ability to write it.

Secondly, for some unexplainable reason, God has filled the hearts of my wife and I with a deep desire to help people see the context of where the Bible took place. Of course, we know this desire is none other than God's sovereign work and grace. It's been a rich joy to have a small part in working with God's grace to provide this book.

What you as a reader find useful in this book, please give the glory and credit to God. What you find that is not useful or to your liking, please place the blame on the author.

Thirdly, I would like to thank my lovely wife, Letsy, for doing much of the research on the secondary "Other Sites of Interest" at the end of each section of the book. Significant time and effort were spent investigating these places.

Lastly, I'd like to thank my son, Joel, for helping with formatting, layout, and proofreading. He was a real trooper, and his contribution was invaluable.

My prayer is that God might use this book in your life to deepen your faith, your understanding of who God is, and how He has used the land of Israel and its people to communicate His eternal message to the world.

Israel: Land of the Bible

The Bible is not a fairy tale written in an unknown time, in an unreal place, and with unreal people. On the contrary, the Bible was written in real-time, in a real place, and with real people. The better we understand the context of the time, place, and people of the Bible, the better we will understand the Bible itself. In other words, by understanding the **world of the Bible** better, we can understand the **words of the Bible** better.

For a person of faith whose beliefs are engrained in the Bible, there is no place on earth like the Holy Land. In this narrow strip of land that connects the three major continents of Africa, Asia, and Europe, God sovereignly placed the land of Israel. It lies on the crossroads of the world and has affected virtually every civilization on earth.

From its barren hills and fertile plains, a message went out from a tethered and worn prophet that still applies today: *"... and many peoples shall come, and say, 'Come, let us go up to the Mountain of the Lord, to the House of the God of Jacob; that He may teach us His ways and that we may walk in His paths. For out of Zion will go forth the law, and the word of the Lord from Jerusalem'"* (Isaiah 2:3–4).

Located on a tiny land bridge between Africa and Asia, there were few travel options between the two continents except through Israel. Therefore, whoever wanted to trade between the two continents, or control the known world, had to conquer and control Israel. For this reason, there have been more wars and conflicts in Israel than in any other country on earth. God positioned Israel in this unique location so He could influence the world and be on "Center Stage." In so doing, God's message of who He is, and His message of salvation and hope, is reaching the entire world.

For nearly 2,000 years, pilgrims of faith have come from all over the world to visit and experience the Holy Land, the land of their spiritual heritage. With Bibles in hand, these pilgrims have walked where Jesus walked and prayed in the places He preached and prayed. For Christians, there is just simply no place like Israel. As we traverse and experience the Holy Land, the better we understand Israel's land, places, and people. This great privilege allows us to better understand God's message written to us on the holy pages of Scripture, and as a result, live lives that glorify and fulfill God's purpose for our existence.

This book is divided into two main sections:

1. Sea of Galilee Sites
2. Northern Israel Sites

Each section is arranged in alphabetical order for your convenience.

Sea of Galilee Sites

Sea of Galilee Overview

Location

1. The Sea of Galilee is located in the northern part of Israel, known as the Galilee region. Therefore, it's called the Sea of Galilee.
2. It's also referred to in Scripture by other names like Ginnosar, Lake of Gennesar, Gennesaret, Sea of Chinneroth, Kinneret, and Sea of Tiberias.

3. It's about 70 miles (115 km.) north of Jerusalem and about 27 miles (45 km.) east of the Mediterranean Sea.
4. It's a freshwater lake about 8 miles (13 km.) wide by about 12 miles (19 km.) long and 150 ft. (46 m.) deep.
5. It's located about 700 ft. (213 m.) below sea level.
6. It's a key freshwater source for much of Israel.
7. Because of its location, storms can arise quickly and drop down onto its surface without much warning.
8. The Sea of Galilee was located on a main crossroad of the known world during Christ's ministry on earth. This international highway was called the "Via Maris" (Way of the Sea) and linked travel between the 3 continents of Africa, Asia, and Europe.
9. Travelers from these 3 continents were forced to use this route as there were few other options for traveling to and from each continent. This was so because there was a desert to the east that was impassible due to lack of water, and the Mediterranean Sea was located to the west, which was not a realistic option for travel as it was expensive and ships were scarce.
10. The Via Maris passed right along the northern shore of the Sea of Galilee, and there are old ruins and markers showing its existence.
11. The north shore of the Sea of Galilee was even more traveled than the roads and routes leading through Jerusalem.

12. Oftentimes, we might think Christ was hiding out somewhere in a remote location. However, just the opposite was true. He chose the northern shore of the Sea of Galilee (and Capernaum was located at a key place along this route) as a center stage so His message would reach as many people as possible in the world.

13. By spending most of His ministry time in the northern Galilee area, Christ's miracles would travel by word of mouth to the ends of the earth. This laid the groundwork and sowed the seeds of the gospel to the rest of the known world so the evangelization work done later by the apostles would be easier and more acceptable to those who heard the message about Christ.

Sea of Galilee from Mt. Arbel

Historical Background

1. Abraham entered the Promised Land through the gateway of the Sea of Galilee when he first journeyed from Ur of the Chaldeans.
2. In Matthew 4, we find that Jesus established his home ministry base in the town of Capernaum, which is located on the northern shore of the Sea of Galilee.
3. At least 6 of the 12 disciples were from right around the Sea of Galilee. These were Peter, Andrew, James, John, Matthew, and Philip.
4. According to Acts 1:11, the rest of the disciples were from the Galilee area as well.

Places of Interest

Listed clockwise, starting at Tiberias

1. Tiberias
2. Mount Arbel – Likely place the Great Commission was given.

Sea of Galilee Sites

3. Magdala – Hometown of Mary Magdalene, from whom Christ cast out 7 demons.
4. Yigal Allon Center – Jesus Boat Museum
5. Calling of the disciples.
6. Tel Chinnereth (Kinneret) – Identified as the biblical city listed by Joshua as one of the fortified cities in the Naftali tribe region (Josh. 19).

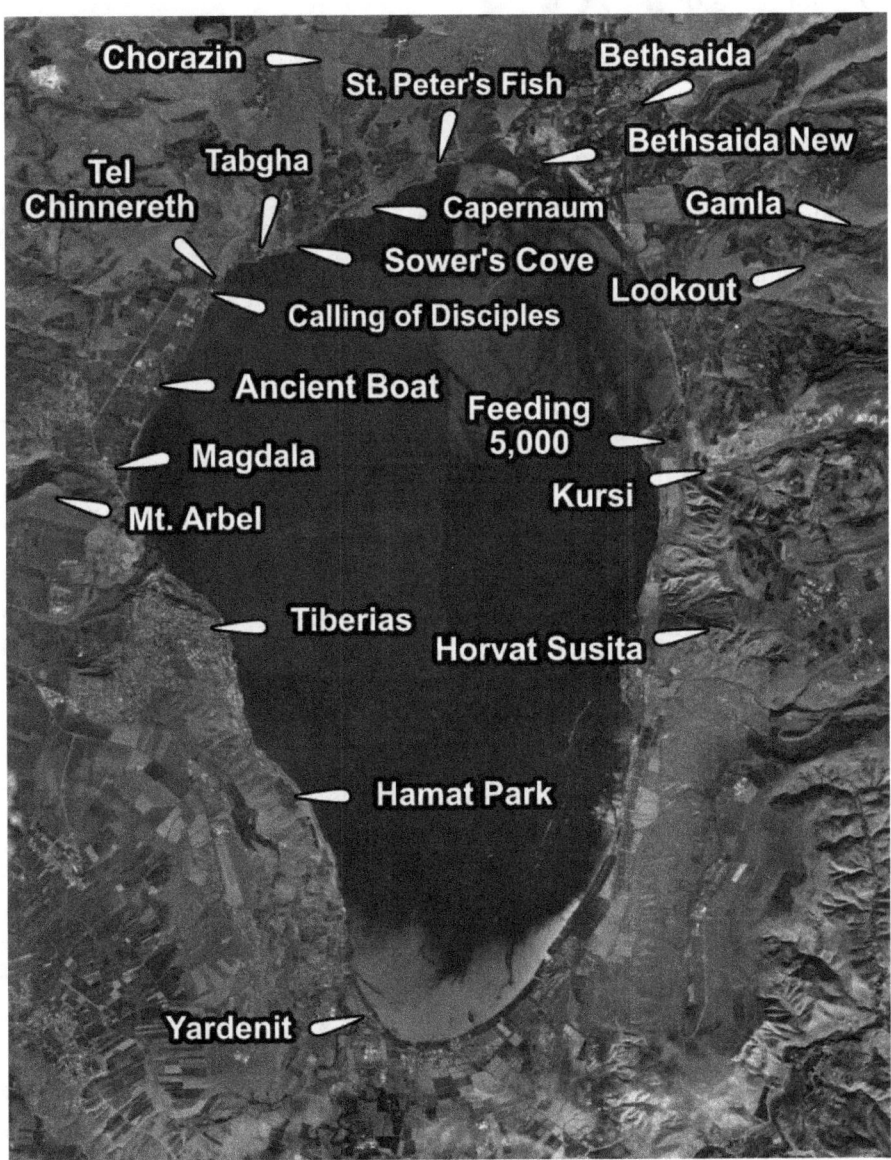

Sea of Galilee & Northern Biblical Sites Guide

7. Tabgha – Restoration of Peter: Church of the Primacy of Saint Peter
8. Tabgha: Church of the Loaves and Fish – The traditional site of the feeding of the 5,000.
9. Mount of Beatitudes – Place from where Christ preached the Sermon on the Mount.
10. Chorazin – One of the 3 towns Jesus cursed because of their unbelief.
11. Sower's Cove – Likely place Christ preached the Parables of the Kingdom sermon.
12. Capernaum – Homebase of Jesus, Franciscan Site

Synagogue at Capernaum

13. Capernaum – Homebase of Jesus, Greek Orthodox Site
14. Capernaum National Park and Peer – Great place to get out into the Sea of Galilee a bit.
15. St. Peter's Fish Restaurant Mifratz-Amnun – Nice restaurant and beach location.
16. Bethsaida traditional location.
17. Bethsaida newly discovered location – New archaeological evidence points to this place as the real Bethsaida.
18. Gamla – Place many Jews jumped to their deaths fleeing the Romans in 67 AD.
19. Sea of Galilee lookout place.
20. Kursi – Demon possessed man healed. Pigs run down a steep slope into the sea just south of Kursi.
21. Feeding of the 5,000 – The most accurate location according to Scripture.
22. Horvat Susita – Old Roman City atop of a hill on the east side of the Sea of Galilee.
23. Yardenit – Nice baptismal site and souvenir store.

Sea of Galilee Sites

24. Hamat Tiberias National Park – Old Ruins of ancient Tiberias.

The Sea of Galilee in the Bible

1. Jesus calmed the sea here two times.
2. Christ fed 5,000 and 4,000 on its eastern shores.
3. Christ walked on water in the northern part of the sea.
4. Christ preached the Sermon on the Mount here, which is His most famous and longest sermon.
5. Jesus cast demons out of a herd of 2,000 pigs here.
6. Christ did the majority of his miracles here in this region.
7. The miraculous "Catch of Fish" was performed here by Jesus.

Boat dock at Capernaum National Park

8. Jesus performed every class of miracle to show He was Lord of every aspect of creation. Here are the kinds of miracles Christ performed:
   - He healed all kinds of sickness.
   - He had power over the demons and the demonic world.
   - He had power over the weather and calmed the sea.
   - He had power over nature and cursed a fig tree, and it died.
   - He had power over animals – He cast demons into a herd of swine, performed miraculous catches of fish, and rode into Jerusalem on an untamed donkey.
   - He had power over food – He fed 5,000 and 4,000 people.
   - He had power over death – He raised a number of people from the dead and rose from the dead Himself.
   - Jesus had power to forgive sins (Mark 2:10).
9. Christ preached the Parables of the Kingdom from its shore.

10. Jesus spent around 50–70% of His ministry time on earth around the Sea of Galilee.
11. The cursing of the unrepentant cities of Chorazin, Bethsaida, and Capernaum was pronounced here by Jesus.
12. The Great Commission was likely given on Mount Arbel, which is the tallest mountain around the Sea of Galilee and has the best view.
13. Jesus appeared here to the disciples after His resurrection.
14. Jesus restored Peter to ministry here.
15. Thirty-four times in the Gospels it's mentioned that multitudes of people followed Jesus. These great crowds could have easily reached 15,000 or more in size.

Matthew 4:23–25: *And he went throughout all Galilee, teaching in their synagogues and proclaiming the gospel of the kingdom and healing every disease and every affliction among the people. 24 So his fame spread throughout all Syria, and they brought him all the sick, those*

Kursi: Demon possessed man healed here

afflicted with various diseases and pains, those oppressed by demons, those having seizures, and paralytics, and he healed them. 25 And **great crowds** *followed him from Galilee and the Decapolis, and from Jerusalem and Judea, and from beyond the Jordan.*

Mark 6:30–34: *The apostles gathered together with Jesus; and they reported to Him all that they had done and taught. 31 And He said to them, "Come away by yourselves to a secluded place and rest a while." (For there were many people coming and going, and they did not even have time to eat.) 32 They went away in the boat to a secluded place by themselves. 33 The people saw them going, and many recognized them and ran there together on foot from all the cities and got there ahead of them. 34 When Jesus went ashore, He saw* **a large crowd**, *and He felt compassion for them because they were like sheep without a shepherd; and He began to teach them* *many things.*

Faith Lesson from the Sea of Galilee

1. Christ chose to locate His ministry base in Capernaum which was on the Via Maris so He would have maximum impact on a worldwide scale. Do we position ourselves to have maximum impact regarding the ministries we are involved in?
2. Jesus performed every class of miracle to show He was Lord of every aspect of creation. Do we believe Jesus was fully God and fully man at the same time?
3. Christ cursed the 3 towns of Capernaum, Chorazin, and Bethsaida because they heard so much teaching and witnessed many miracles but grew apathetic and hardhearted. Are we becoming apathetic toward Christ and His Word in our own personal lives?
4. Christ gave the Great Commission overlooking the Sea of Galilee. Are we seriously fulfilling the Great Commission, or have we become lazy and apathetic to this key command?

Sea of Galilee at sunset

Journal/Notes

Bethsaida

Location

1. Currently, there are two leading candidates for the true Bethsaida location. The first is the traditional site that has been excavated from 1987 to the present. It sits upon a hill and is located about 1.5 miles or 2.25 km. from the highwater mark of the Sea of Galilee. Because there were no other sites excavated besides this first site, it became the default site. The traditional site is known as Et Tell.

   A new site called El Araj has been recently excavated since 2014, and all the evidence points to it as the best candidate for the true Bethsaida location. It is located at the high-water mark on the northeast side of the Sea of Galilee at the inlet of the Jordan River and fits the biblical and historical records much better than the traditional site.

2. We know from the Bible that Bethsaida was in a desolate, remote place with little population.

   Luke 9:10: *The apostles, when they had returned, told him what things they had done. He took them, and withdrew apart to a **deserted place** of a city called Bethsaida.*

3. The northwestern side of the Sea of Galilee was densely populated in Jesus' time, but the northeastern side where Bethsaida was located was desolate.

4. Bethsaida was a fishing village right on the seashore of the Sea of Galilee. In fact, its name means "House of Fishing."

5. In John 1:44, we find that at least 3 disciples were from here: *Now **Philip** was from **Bethsaida**, the city of **Andrew** and **Peter**.*

   We also know that at least Peter and Andrew were fishermen, so they lived in Bethsaida to be close to the sea.

6. As mentioned, the traditional site of Bethsaida is located 1.5 miles (2.25 km.) from the Sea of Galilee.
   - This presents a challenge as Bethsaida was a fishing village right on the Sea of Galilee.
   - Some have suggested the water level was higher back in Jesus' day, but this cannot be true as Capernaum, Magdala, and other towns are right on the sea. If the water level had been higher, these other towns could not have existed.
   - Pliny the Elder, a first-century Roman writer, called Bethsaida *"One of four lovely cities on the Sea of Galilee."*

Historical Background

1. Bethsaida was a fishing village with several hundred inhabitants during the time of Christ.
2. At least 3 of the 12 disciples were from Bethsaida.

John 1:44: *Now **Philip** was from Bethsaida, of the city of **Andrew** and **Peter**.*

Traditional site of Bethsaida

3. Later on, however, these disciples moved to Capernaum to be closer to where Jesus lived.

Mark 1:21: *And they went into **Capernaum**, and immediately on the Sabbath, he entered the synagogue and was teaching.*

Mark 1:28: *And immediately he left the synagogue and entered the house of Simon and Andrew, with James and John. And at once his fame spread everywhere throughout all the surrounding region of Galilee.*

Places of Interest

1. Et-Tell site of Bethsaida – Traditional Location
2. El Araj site of Bethsaida – New Location
3. Feeding of the 5,000

4. Approximate place Jesus walked on water.
5. Capernaum

Bethsaida in the Bible

1. **Philip, Andrew, and Peter were from Bethsaida (John 1:44).**
2. **Jesus healed a blind man at Bethsaida.**

   Mark 8:22–25: *And they came to **Bethsaida**. And some people brought to him a blind man and begged him to touch him. 23 And he took the blind man by the hand and led him out of the village, and when he had spit on his eyes and laid his hands on him, he asked him, "Do you see anything?" 24 And he looked up and said, "I see people, but they look like trees, walking." 25 Then Jesus laid his hands on his eyes again; and he opened his eyes, his sight was restored, and he saw everything clearly.*

3. **Bethsaida was one of the 3 towns Jesus cursed because of their unbelief in Him after witnessing all His miracles.**

   Matthew 11:21: *Woe to you, Chorazin! Woe to you, **Bethsaida**! For if the mighty works had been done in Tyre and Sidon which were done in you, they would have repented long ago in sackcloth and* *ashes.*

4. **It was close to Bethsaida, where Christ fed the 5,000.**

   Luke 9:10–17: *When the apostles returned, they gave an account to Him of all that they had done. Taking them with Him, He withdrew by Himself to a city called* **Bethsaida**. *11 But the crowds were aware of this and followed Him; and welcoming them, He began speaking to them about the kingdom of God and curing those who had need of healing. 12 Now the day was ending, and the twelve came and said to Him, "Send the crowd away, that they may go into the surrounding villages and countryside and find lodging and get something to eat; for here we are in a desolate place." But he said to them, "You*

   New location of Bethsaida

   give them something to eat." They said, "We have no more than five loaves and two fish—unless we are to go and buy food for all these people." 14 For there were about five thousand men. And he said to his disciples, "Have them sit down in groups of about fifty each." 15 And they did so, and had them all sit down. 16 And taking the five loaves and the two fish, he looked up to heaven and said a blessing over them. Then he broke the loaves and gave them to the disciples to set before the crowd. 17 And they all ate and were satisfied. And what was left over was picked up, twelve baskets of broken pieces.

5. **Not far from Bethsaida, Jesus walked on water and calmed the sea.**

   Mark 6:45–51: *Immediately he made his disciples get into the boat and go before him to the other side, to* **Bethsaida**, *while he dismissed the crowd. 46 And after he had taken leave of them, he went up on the mountain to pray. 47 And when evening came, the boat was out on the sea, and he was alone on the land. 48 And he saw that they were making headway painfully, for the wind was against them. And about the fourth watch of the night [the last watch before dawn], he came to them, walking on the sea. He meant to pass by them, 49 but when they saw him walking on the sea, they* *thought it was a ghost, and cried out, 50 for they all saw him and were terrified. But immediately he spoke to them and said, "Take heart; it is I. Do not be afraid." 51 And he got into the boat with them, and the wind ceased. And they were utterly astounded.*

Faith Lesson from Bethsaida

1. Like the healing of the blind man, Jesus often heals in different and strange ways. Do we have faith and trust in God regardless of how or if He chooses to heal?
2. Christ cursed the town of Bethsaida because its inhabitants were apathetic, showed unbelief in Christ, and chose not to follow and obey Him. Are we often slow to trust and obey Christ as well?
3. Christ fed the 5,000 in the area of Bethsaida to reveal He was the true bread of life from heaven and that His Word is our spiritual food. In the same way there were 12 baskets of food left over, Christ, as our Bread from Heaven, is also abundant and overflowing in feeding us spiritual food through His Word. Are we eating daily and finding our life from the true Bread of Life?

Ruins at new Bethsaida location

4. Not far from Bethsaida Jesus walked on water and calmed the sea. Am I finding rest and peace in Jesus in the midst of my personal storms of life?

Isaiah 26:3–4: *You keep him in perfect peace whose mind is stayed on you, because he trusts in you. 4 Trust in the Lord forever, for the Lord God is an everlasting rock.*

Journal/Notes:

Sea of Galilee Sites

Calling of the Disciples

Location

It's very likely that the biblical account of the calling of at least 6 of the 12 disciples occurred on the northern shore of the Sea of Galilee. This was the area where most of the fishing was done, and the fishing towns were located.

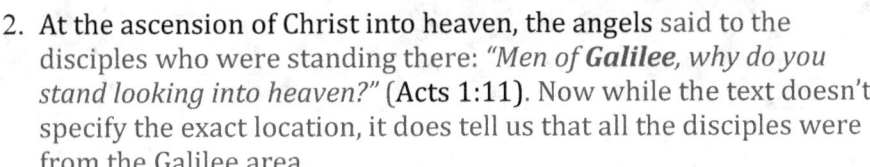

Historical Background

1. While the Bible clearly mentions that 6 of the 12 disciples were from the Sea of Galilee, it's possible more were from this area as well.
2. At the ascension of Christ into heaven, the angels said to the disciples who were standing there: *"Men of **Galilee**, why do you stand looking into heaven?"* (**Acts 1:11**). Now while the text doesn't specify the exact location, it does tell us that all the disciples were from the Galilee area.

Places of Interest

1. Northern Shore of the Sea of Galilee
2. Most likely place several of the disciples were called.
3. Gennesaret
4. Magdala
5. Tabgha
6. Capernaum
7. Bethsaida
8. Sea of Galilee

Calling of the Disciples in the Bible

1. **It appears by looking at the biblical narrative that Jesus had several contacts with some of the disciples before His final call for them to leave everything and follow Him.**

   John 1:35–44: *The next day again John was standing with two of his disciples, 36 and he looked at Jesus as he walked by and said, "Behold, the Lamb of God!" 37 The two disciples heard him say this, and they followed Jesus. 38 Jesus turned and saw them following and said to them, "What are you seeking?" And they said to him, "Rabbi" (which means Teacher), "where are you staying?" 39 He said to them, "Come and you will see." So they came and saw where he was staying, and they stayed with him that day, for it was about the tenth hour. 40 One of the two who heard John speak and followed Jesus was **Andrew**, Simon Peter's brother. 41 He first found his own brother **Simon** and said to him, "We have found the Messiah" (which means Christ). 42 He brought him to Jesus. Jesus looked at him and said, "So you are Simon the son of John? You shall be called Cephas"* (which means Peter). 43 The next day Jesus decided to go to Galilee. He found **Philip** and said to him, "Follow me." 44 Now Philip was from Bethsaida, the city of Andrew and Peter.

2. **In the following passage, we see what appears to be a final contact with some of the disciples before Jesus' last call for them to follow Him in full-time ministry.**

   Luke 5:1–11: *On one occasion, while the crowd was pressing in on him to hear the word of God, he was standing by the lake of Gennesaret, 2 and he saw two boats by the lake, but the fishermen had gone out of them and were washing their nets. 3 Getting into one of the boats, which was* **Simon's***, he asked him to put out a little from the land. And he sat down and taught the people from the boat. 4 And when he had finished speaking, he said to Simon, "Put out into the deep and let down your*

   Northwestern shore of the Sea of Galilee

   nets for a catch." 5 And Simon answered, "Master, we toiled all night and took nothing! But at your word I will let down the nets." 6 And when they had done this, they enclosed a large number of fish, and their nets were breaking. 7 They signaled to their partners in the other boat to come and help them. And they came and filled both the boats, so that they began to sink. 8 But when Simon Peter saw it, he fell down at Jesus' knees, saying, "Depart from me, for I am a sinful man, O Lord." 9 For he and all who were with him were astonished at the catch of fish that they had taken, 10 and so also were **James** *and* **John***, sons of Zebedee, who were partners with* **Simon***. And Jesus said to Simon, "Do not be afraid; from now on you will be catching men." 11 And when they had brought their boats to land, they left everything and followed him.*

3. **The calling of Matthew, the tax collector.**

   Matthew 9:9: *As Jesus passed on from there, he saw a man called* **Matthew** *sitting at the tax booth, and he said to him, "Follow* me." And he rose and followed him.

From Matthew 9:1, we see that the calling of Matthew was close to Capernaum, which is on the northern shore of the Sea of Galilee.

Faith Lesson from the Calling of the Disciples

1. When God calls us to salvation or a certain calling or task, this might sometimes involve a process and have several confirmations. Are you genuinely saved? Is there some special calling or mission you are sensing from the Lord?
2. God wants our complete devotion and obedience. He doesn't want us to add Him onto our lives and make Him an accessory that we go to just when we need help. God refuses to be an ATM. Do I follow Jesus for His blessings only, or am I willing to deny myself and suffer for Him as well?
3. God calls us to be His disciples and devote our entire life to Him. Luke 14:25–27, 33: *Now great crowds accompanied him, and he turned and said to them, 26 "If anyone comes to me and does not hate his own father and mother and wife and children and brothers and sisters, yes, and even his own life, he cannot be my disciple. 27 Whoever does not bear his own cross and come after me cannot be my disciple. 33 So therefore, any one of you who does not renounce all that he has cannot be my disciple."*

Northern shore of the Sea of Galilee

4. Am I willing to love Christ and follow Him regardless of the cost?
5. In comparison to my love for Christ, all other relationships should fade. The contrast here is that compared to my love for Christ, all other relationships would seem like hate in comparison. Do all my relationships appear as hate in comparison to my love for Christ?

6. Christ said that there would be a great falling away from the faith in the last days, and there would be many false teachers. Unfortunately, in many churches today, a soft version of the gospel is proclaimed. They neglect to emphasize repentance, the judgments of God, the true cost of discipleship, service, and sacrifice. Instead, there is an overemphasis on the blessings of God and how He exists to serve our needs and make us happy rather than us serving Him and finding true joy in our devotion to Him. This soft gospel will likely lead to the great apostasy mentioned in Scripture.

Northern shore of the Sea of Galilee

7. Am I growing deeper in my knowledge of God's Word so I don't fall into the many traps that will lead to the great apostasy of the last days?

Journal/Notes:

Capernaum

Location

1. Capernaum is located on the north shore of the Sea of Galilee.

2. It was located on the Via Maris, which was the main international highway of the known world during the time of Christ.

   - The Via Maris linked the three continents of Africa, Asia, and Europe.
   - Travelers were forced to use this route as there were few other options for traveling to and from each continent.
   - The north shore of the Sea of Galilee was even more traveled than the roads and routes leading through Jerusalem.
   - It might appear that Christ set up His ministry base in a remote place. However, just the opposite is true. He chose the northern shore of the Sea of Galilee (and Capernaum was located at a key place along the Via Maris) as a center stage so His message would reach as many people as possible throughout the world.
   - By spending most of His ministry time in the northern Galilee area, Christ's miracles traveled by word of mouth to the ends of the earth. This laid the groundwork and sowed the seeds of the gospel to the rest of the known world. As a result, evangelism done later on by the apostles would be easier and more acceptable.

3. Today, Capernaum is shared between two sites. The Franciscan site receives around 90% of visitors as it possesses the synagogue, Peter's home, village ruins, ancient artifacts, and nice access to the beach. The Greek Orthodox site has chosen to remain basically unexcavated and serene.

Sea of Galilee Sites

Historical Background

1. The name Capernaum is derived from two words, *Caper*, which means village, and *Naum*, which is from the title, Nahum. Therefore, some believe that the town was named after the Prophet Nahum.
2. Capernaum was a fishing village with a population of around 1,000 during the time of Christ.
3. Capernaum became the hometown of Jesus after moving from his boyhood home of Nazareth. It also became the ministry headquarters of Christ during His ministry on earth.

Matthew 4:13–17: *And leaving Nazareth he went and lived in **Capernaum** by the sea, in the territory of Zebulun and Naphtali, 14 so that what was spoken by the prophet Isaiah might be fulfilled: 15 "The land of Zebulun and the land of Naphtali, the way of the sea, beyond the Jordan, Galilee of the Gentiles— 16 the people dwelling in darkness have seen a great light, and for those dwelling in the region and shadow of death, on them a light has dawned." 17 From that time Jesus began to preach, saying, "Repent, for the kingdom of heaven is at hand."*

Capernaum: Franciscan site

4. Capernaum is mentioned more than any other town around the Sea of Galilee.
5. Capernaum was also the home of Peter, James, Andrew, John, and Matthew.
6. The Synagogue in Capernaum was built by a Roman Centurion of whom Jesus healed his servant.

Luke 7:5: *For he loves our nation, and he is the one **who built us our synagogue.***

7. The synagogue that existed during Christ's time is made from black basalt stone, and its foundations are under the current synagogue built out of limestone.

Sea of Galilee & Northern Biblical Sites Guide

8. The current synagogue was built in the 4th century and was quite luxurious and impressive. This happened because Capernaum became a venerated site due to its role as the ministry base and home of Jesus and other apostles.
9. Information about Peter's home.
   - Many substantial archaeological excavations have verified the location of Peter's home.
   - There have been several churches built over Peter's home throughout the centuries.
   - The early Christian believers first built a building over Peter's house in around 50 AD.
   - Peter's home was where Jesus also lived. It contained the central kitchen and living quarters (which are preserved today) and then individual bedrooms connected to it.
   - In the 5th century AD, an octagon-shaped church was built over Peter's house.
   - Recently, in 1990, a church was built over the previous ruins of Peter's house. You can walk inside it and look down at the ruins through a glass floor in the church.

Sea of Galilee Sites

10. At the Greek Orthodox site of Capernaum, the Greek Orthodox Church was built in 1931 and dedicated to the twelve apostles.

Places of Interest

1. Capernaum Franciscan Site
   - Synagogue
   - Peter's Home
   - Village Houses
   - Ancient Artifacts
   - Pillar inscribed with the name of a family (Alphaeus) mentioned in Mark 2:13.
   - Via Maris Roman Road Post Marker
2. Capernaum Greek Orthodox Site
3. Capernaum National Park – Has a peer, which is a great place to walk out onto the Sea of Galilee.

Capernaum in the Bible

1. **Christ left Nazareth to live and set up His ministry base in Capernaum.**

   Matthew 4:13: *And leaving Nazareth he went and lived in **Capernaum** by the sea, in the territory of Zebulun and Naphtali.*

2. **Jesus frequently taught in the Synagogue in Capernaum.**

   Mark 1:21–28: *And they went into **Capernaum**, and immediately on the Sabbath, he entered the synagogue and **was teaching**. 22 And they were astonished at his teaching, for he taught them as one who had authority, and not as the scribes. 23 And immediately there was in their synagogue a man with an unclean spirit. And he cried out, 24 "What have you to do with us, Jesus of Nazareth? Have you come to destroy us? I know who you*

   Capernaum: Greek Orthodox site

   are—the Holy One of God." 25 But Jesus rebuked him, saying, "Be silent, and come out of him!" 26 And the unclean spirit, convulsing him and crying out with a loud voice, came out of him. 27 And they were all amazed, so that they questioned among themselves, saying, "What is this? A new teaching with authority! He commands even the unclean spirits, and they obey him." 28 And at once his fame spread everywhere throughout all the surrounding region of Galilee.

3. **Jesus healed Peter's mother and many others in Capernaum.**

   Mark 1:29–34: *And immediately he left the synagogue and entered the house of Simon and Andrew, with James and John. 30 Now Simon's mother-in-law lay ill with a fever, and immediately they told him about her. 31 And he came and took her by the hand and lifted her up, and the fever left her, and she began to serve them. 32 That evening at sundown they brought to him all who were sick or oppressed by demons. 33 And the whole city was gathered together at the door. 34 And he healed many who were sick with various diseases, and cast out many demons. And he would not permit the demons to speak, because they knew him.*

4. **In Capernaum, Jesus forgave and healed a paralyzed man. This likely happened right at the home where Jesus lived.**

   Mark 2:1–5: *And when he returned to Capernaum after some days, it was reported that he was at home. 2 And many were gathered together, so that there was no more room, not even at the door. And he was preaching the word to them. 3 And they came, bringing to him a paralytic carried by four men. 4 And when they could not get near him because of the crowd, they removed the roof above him, and when they had made an opening, they let down the bed on which the paralytic lay. 5 And when Jesus saw their faith, he said to the paralytic, "Son, your sins are forgiven."*

5. **Christ marveled at the great faith of a centurion in Capernaum.**

   Luke 7:1–10: *After he had finished all his sayings in the hearing of the people, he entered* **Capernaum**. *2 Now a centurion had a servant who was sick and at the point of death, who was highly valued by him. 3 When the centurion heard about Jesus, he*

   Synagogue at Franciscan site

   sent to him elders of the Jews, asking him to come and heal his servant. 4 And when they came to Jesus, they pleaded with him earnestly, saying, "He is worthy to have you do this for him, 5 for he loves our nation, and he is the one who built us our synagogue." 6 And Jesus went with them. When he was not far from the house, the centurion sent friends, saying to him, "Lord, do not trouble yourself, for I am not worthy to have you come under my roof. 7 Therefore I did not presume to come to you. But say the word, and let my servant be healed. 8 For I too am a man set under authority, with soldiers under me: and I say to one, 'Go,' and he goes; and to another, 'Come,' and he comes; and to my servant, 'Do this,' and he does it." 9 When Jesus heard these things, he marveled at him, and turning to the crowd that followed him, said, "I tell you, not even in Israel have I found such faith." 10 And when those who had been sent returned to the house, they found the servant well.

6. **The Parables of the Kingdom were preached close to Capernaum.**

   Matthew 13:1–3: *That same day Jesus went out of the house and sat by the lake. 2 Such large crowds gathered around him that he got into a boat and sat in it, while all the people stood on the shore. 3 And He spoke many things to them in parables.*

7. **The miracle of Peter getting money out of the mouth of a fish to pay the temple tax for himself and Jesus happened in Capernaum.**

Capernaum

   Matthew 17:24–27: *When they came to **Capernaum**, the collectors of the two-drachma tax went up to Peter and said, "Does your teacher not pay the tax?" 25 He said, "Yes." And when he came into the house, Jesus spoke to him first, saying, "What do you think, Simon? From whom do kings of the earth take toll or tax? From their sons or from others?" 26 And when he said, "From others," Jesus said to him, "Then the sons are free. 27 However, not to give offense to them, go to the sea and cast a hook and take the first fish that comes up, and when you open its mouth, you will find a shekel. Take that and give it to them for me and for yourself."*

8. **Jesus called Matthew, the tax collector, close to Capernaum.**

   Matthew 9:9: *As Jesus passed on from there [Capernaum], he saw a man called Matthew sitting at the tax booth, and he said to him, "Follow me." And he rose and followed him.*

9. **Capernaum was one of the 3 towns Christ cursed because of their unbelief in Him.**

   Matthew 11:23–24: *And you, Capernaum, will you be exalted to heaven? You will be brought down to Hades. For if the mighty works done in you had been done in Sodom, it would have remained until this day. 24 But I tell you that it will be more tolerable on the Day of Judgment for the land of Sodom than for you.*

Sea of Galilee Sites

Faith Lesson from Capernaum

1. Christ astonished the large crowds who followed him because He taught with authority. He was completely different from all other teachers because He was God in the flesh. Are we astonished today as we read Christ's teachings in His Word?

2. Christ healed multitudes of people in and around Capernaum. He also showed He was God as He forgave their sins. Forgiving sins is something only God can do. Do we believe Christ was God in the flesh and full deity?

Peter's home – Likely place Jesus lived

3. Christ marveled at the great faith of a Roman Centurion. Do we trust God in such a way that He would marvel at our faith?

4. Unfortunately, Christ cursed the town of Capernaum because of their unbelief in Him. After all they had seen, and after many of them had been healed by Jesus, they were still filled with unbelief. Unbelief is, therefore, a sin. Do we have unbelief in Christ and who He claimed to be? Do we also have unbelief in trusting Him in our daily lives when things don't seem to make sense?

Journal/Notes:

Chorazin

Location

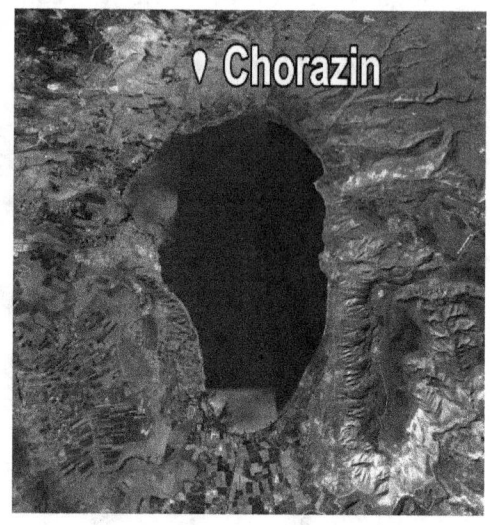

1. Chorazin (Korazim) is located about 2 miles (3 km.) north of the Sea of Galilee.
2. From Chorazin, you can see the Sea of Galilee, Bethsaida, and some of Capernaum.
3. It's located a little off the beaten path.
4. It was built out of black basalt stone, which was common in the Galilee area.
5. The construction of the homes in Chorazin are quite well preserved and show how the home where Jesus lived in Capernaum might have looked.
6. The walls of the homes consisted of stone, and the roofs were of either mud bricks or branches and leaves.
7. This area is very dry, and the water supply was essential for sustaining life in this town. A spring is located on the north-east side of the town, which was the source of the city's water, in addition to the cisterns under the houses.
8. In the time of Jesus, Chorazin was about 15 acres (7 hectares) in size and had an estimated population of around 500–1,000.

Historical Background

1. Chorazin was one of the 3 towns (Chorazin, Bethsaida, and Capernaum), which made up what scholars call "The Evangelical Triangle."
2. Jesus set up His home ministry base in Capernaum, which was nearby to Chorazin.
3. Jesus spent around 50-70% of His ministry time around the northern shore of the Sea of Galilee, so those in Chorazin would

Sea of Galilee Sites

have repeatedly heard and seen all He did.

4. A tree with the kind of thorns that would have been used for the crown of thorns Jesus wore at His crucifixion can be found here.

Places of Interest

1. Synagogue
   - Most of the ruins seen today are from the 3rd century.
   - Jesus would have taught here frequently.
   - It has an ornamental shell which would have been the top part of the cabinet where the Torah and Old Testament Scrolls would have been kept.

2. Chair of Moses
   - An unusual find in the ruins of the synagogue was a Seat of Moses carved out of a single basalt block. From it, the Torah would have been read.
   - The chair seen here is a replica of the original one. The original is in a museum in Jerusalem.

- The "Chair of Moses" was a phrase used by Jesus to signify the place of authority that the scribes and Pharisees had in interpreting the Law and exercising their authority over the Jewish people.

    Matthew 23:1–3: *Then Jesus spoke to the crowds and to His disciples, 2 saying: "The scribes and the Pharisees have seated themselves in the **chair of Moses**; 3 therefore all that they tell you, do and observe, but do not do according to their deeds; for they say things and do not do them."*

3. Mikvah Baths
4. Residential Homes
5. Thorn Trees (the kind used for Jesus' crown of thorns)
6. Public Buildings
7. Sea of Galilee

Chorazin in the Bible

1. **Christ pronounced judgment upon the cities and towns that rejected the gospel.**

    Luke 9:1–6: *And He called the twelve together, and gave them power and authority over all the demons and to heal diseases. 2 And He sent them out to proclaim the kingdom of God and to perform healing. 3 And He said to them, "Take nothing for your journey,*

    Synagogue

    *neither a staff, nor a bag, nor bread, nor money; and do not even have two tunics apiece. 4 Whatever house you enter, stay there until you leave that city. 5 And as for those who do not receive you, as you go out from that city, **shake the dust off your feet as a testimony against them**." 6 Departing, they began going throughout the* *villages, preaching the gospel and healing everywhere.*

2. **Jesus cursed those in Chorazin because they rejected Him, His teachings, and the many miracles He had done in their midst.**

   Matthew 11:21–24: *Woe to you, **Chorazin**! Woe to you, Bethsaida! For if the miracles had occurred in Tyre and Sidon which occurred in you, they would have repented long ago in sackcloth and ashes. 22 Nevertheless, I say to you, it will be more tolerable for Tyre and Sidon in the day of judgment than for you. 23 And you, Capernaum, will not be exalted to heaven, will you? You will descend to Hades; for if the miracles had occurred in Sodom which occurred in you, it would have remained to this day. 24 Nevertheless, I say to you that it will be more tolerable for the land of Sodom in the day of judgment, than for you.*

   Chorazin

3. **To whom much is given, much is required.**

   Luke 12:48: *Everyone to whom much was given, of him much will be required, and from him to whom they entrusted much, they will demand the more.*

4. **Instead of being blessed, Chorazin, Bethsaida, and Capernaum chose to be cursed. Today, each town is a testament to God's curse upon them.**

Faith Lesson from Chorazin

1. Chorazin is a testament to Christ's judgment on a people who rejected His teachings, miracles, healing, and salvation. Are we guilty of rejecting Christ and His teachings in some way?
2. Chorazin stands as a warning to us today not to do the same. Are we walking in close obedience, or living in casual obedience to Christ, or even disobedience?

3. In the same way Chorazin lies in ruins, our lives will lie in ruins if we reject Christ and the life He offers. Are we genuinely living for Christ and putting His Word into practice?
4. It appears there will be different degrees of torment and judgment in hell because Christ said it would be more tolerable in the day of judgment for other cities than for Chorazin. What do you think?
5. Following Christ brings life and blessing; rejecting Him brings death and destruction.

Romans 8:6–8: *For the mind set on the flesh is death, but the mind set on the Spirit is life and peace, 7 because the mind set on the flesh is hostile toward God; for it does not subject itself to the law of God, for it is not even able to do so, 8 and those who are in the flesh cannot please God.*

Chair of Moses

Journal/Notes:

Sea of Galilee Sites

Feeding the 5,000

Location

1. The traditional site of this miracle is at Tabgha, located on the northwestern side of the Sea of Galilee.
2. However, we believe this miracle most likely took place on the eastern side of the Sea of Galilee, south of Bethsaida a bit.
3. Scripture says Jesus and His disciples were headed to Bethsaida, a desolate or deserted place (Mark 6:31; Luke 9:10). Tabgha is in a very populated area and on the opposite side of the sea from Bethsaida.

4. The large population area was from Tiberias to Capernaum (the northwestern side). The deserted area was on the northeastern and eastern sides of the sea.
5. Bethsaida was a small fishing village and was about the only town on the northeastern side of the sea.
6. Immediately after feeding the 5,000, Jesus ordered His disciples to cross over to the other side of the sea (Matt. 14:22).
7. While the disciples were crossing over to the other side is when a strong storm arose. Jesus walked on water (Peter attempted to as well), and Jesus calmed the storm.
8. The storm seems to have changed the course of their destination as Scripture says that they ended up arriving in the area of Gennesaret (Matt. 14:34–36).
9. Gennesaret is located on the northwestern side of the sea where all the population is.
10. Gennesaret is less than 2 miles (3 km.) south of Tabgha. If the miracle happened at Tabgha, going from Tabgha to Gennesaret wouldn't be crossing over the other side of the sea as both towns are nearby to each other.

11. After Christ arrived at Gennesaret, many heard he had arrived, and a large multitude gathered for healing. If Christ had just been in the area of Tabgha, it wouldn't make sense that a large crowd would gather again right after Christ had just been there.
12. From the location of the feeding of the 5,000, the disciples headed in the direction toward Bethsaida and Capernaum (Mark 6:45; John 6:16–17). Therefore, they had to be enough south of Bethsaida to head in that direction by boat.

Feeding of the 5,000 in the Bible

13. For these reasons, we believe the best biblical location for the feeding of the multitude is just south of Bethsaida in this open, flat area. It seems to fit the text and the geography of the land best.

Historical Background

1. This miracle happened just after Jesus had sent out the 12 disciples to preach and heal throughout Israel (Luke 9:1–9).
2. You would think after being used so mightily by God that the disciples would have had more faith.
3. It also took place just after the death of John the Baptist (Matt. 14:1–12).
4. Jesus and His disciples were headed to the remote area of Bethsaida to rest after the long ministry period they had just finished (being sent out two by two, preaching and healing).

Mark 6:30–32: *The apostles returned to Jesus and told him all that they had done and taught. 31 And he said to them, "Come away by yourselves to a* **desolate place** *and rest a while." For many were coming and going, and they had no leisure even to eat. 32 And they went away in the boat to a desolate place by themselves.*

5. However, instead of resting, a huge ministry opportunity awaited

Sea of Galilee Sites

them.

Mark 6:33–34: *Now many saw them going and recognized them, and they ran there on foot from all the towns and got there ahead of them. 34 When he went ashore, he saw a great crowd, and he had compassion on them, because they were like sheep without a shepherd. And he began to teach them many things.*

6. Scripture mentions that there were 5,000 who were fed, not including women and children. This means there could easily have been 15,000 people or more present.

Places of Interest

1. Bethsaida
2. Tabgha
3. Gennesaret
4. Tiberias
5. Feeding of the 5,000 Location
6. Arrival and Departure Beach
7. Desolate side of the Sea of Galilee
8. Populated side of the Sea of Galilee
9. Sea of Galilee

1. **Feeding the multitude.**

    Luke 9:10–11: *On their return, the apostles told him all that they had done. And he took them and withdrew apart to a town called* **Bethsaida**. *11 When the crowds learned it, they followed him, and he welcomed them and spoke to them of the kingdom of God and cured those who had need of healing.*

    Luke 9:12–17: *Now the day began to wear away, and the twelve came and said to him, "Send the crowd away to go into the surrounding villages and countryside to find lodging and get provisions, for we are here in a* **desolate place***." 13 But he said to them, "You give them something to eat." They said, "We have no more than five loaves and two fish—unless we are to go and buy food for all these people." 14 For there were about five thousand men. And he said to his disciples, "Have them sit down in groups of about fifty each." 15 And they did so, and had them all sit down. 16 And taking the five loaves and the two fish, he looked up to heaven and said a blessing over them. Then he broke the loaves and gave them to the disciples to set before the crowd. 17 And they all ate and were satisfied. And what was left over was picked up, twelve baskets of broken pieces.*

2. **Interestingly, there were twelve baskets. This was no accident as there were 12 tribes of Israel and 12 apostles.**
3. **After feeding the 5,000, the disciples encountered a huge storm. Christ walked on water, calmed the storm, and then they arrived on the northwest side of the sea at Gennesaret (Matt. 14:34–36).**
4. **The crowd Jesus fed later approached Jesus to make Him King; however, Jesus rebuked them.**

    John 6:25–27: *When they found him on the other side of the sea, they said to him, "Rabbi, when did you come here?" 26 Jesus answered them, "Truly, truly, I say to you, you are seeking me, not because you saw signs, but because you ate your fill of the loaves. 27 Do not labor for the food that perishes, but for the food that endures to eternal life, which the Son of Man will give to you. For on him God the Father has set his seal."*

Faith Lesson from Feeding the 5,000

1. The disciples should have had more faith after being used mightily by God to preach and heal many people. What about us? Do we lack faith after seeing all God has done for us and others?
2. The crowd later approached Jesus to make Him King. However, Jesus rebuked them because they were just seeking what He could do for them and weren't interested in true discipleship. Do we tend only to want God's blessings but no discipleship, sacrifice, suffering, or persecution?
3. Like the crowd Jesus fed, today, many people come to God for help and want to be fixed up. However, they don't want Christ to be the Lord of their lives. Do we embrace the lordship of Christ, or do we just want our problems solved and then continue living as we please?
4. God also cares for our spiritual needs and likens Himself to spiritual bread. Are you laboring for the bread that endures to eternal life, or are you more focused on temporary things that will soon fade away?
5. Are we feeding our souls daily with God's Word and the Bread of Life?

    John 6:35: *Jesus said to them, "I am the bread of life. The one who comes to me will never become hungry, and the one who believes in me will never become thirsty."*

    Matthew 4:4: *It is written, "Man does not live on bread alone, but on every word that comes from the mouth of God."*

Journal/Notes:

Jesus Walks on the Water, Calms the Storm and Sea

Location

1. This miracle took place in the middle of the widest part of the sea. John 6:19 suggests it was about 3-4 miles (5.5 km.) from the eastern shore. The sea is about 8 miles (13 km.) wide at its widest part, so this would place them in the middle of the sea.
2. They were also a long way from land (Matt. 14:24). This means they were a long way from the northern part of the seashore as well.

Historical Background

1. The disciples had just come off an amazing time of preaching and healing all throughout Israel (Christ had sent them out two by two).
2. Jesus took them to the eastern side of the sea, south of Bethsaida, to rest. However, instead of resting, a large crowd gathered, and Jesus taught them all day and then fed them. There were 5,000 men, not counting women and children present, which means there were probably 15,000–20,000 people or more total.
3. After Christ fed the multitude, they wanted to make Him King by force (John 6:15). However, what they had in mind was an earthly kingdom wherein the Romans would be overthrown, and Jesus would return them to their glory days. This was prophesied in Scripture, but Christ's earthly kingdom would not be realized until His second coming.
4. The disciples were caught up in the frenzy of the crowd's desire to make Jesus King, so He immediately sent them away by boat to the other side of the sea.

Sea of Galilee Sites

5. The disciple's hearts were hard, and Scripture says they didn't learn anything from the feeding of the 5,000 (Matt. 16:5–12).
6. After feeding the 5,000, Jesus went up on a mountain to pray. He likely prayed that His disciples would learn the lesson of faith He was about to teach them. This lesson would involve sending a storm and revealing His deity to them.
7. Jesus purposefully allowed them to get to a state of utter disaster, fear, and desperation, so what He was about to teach them would sink in deeply.
8. The narrative of Scripture would place the disciples sailing from the eastern shore of the Sea of Galilee to the western shore.

Places of Interest

1. Feeding of the 5,000 Location
2. Mountain upon which Jesus prayed.
3. Departure Beach
4. Bethsaida
5. Capernaum

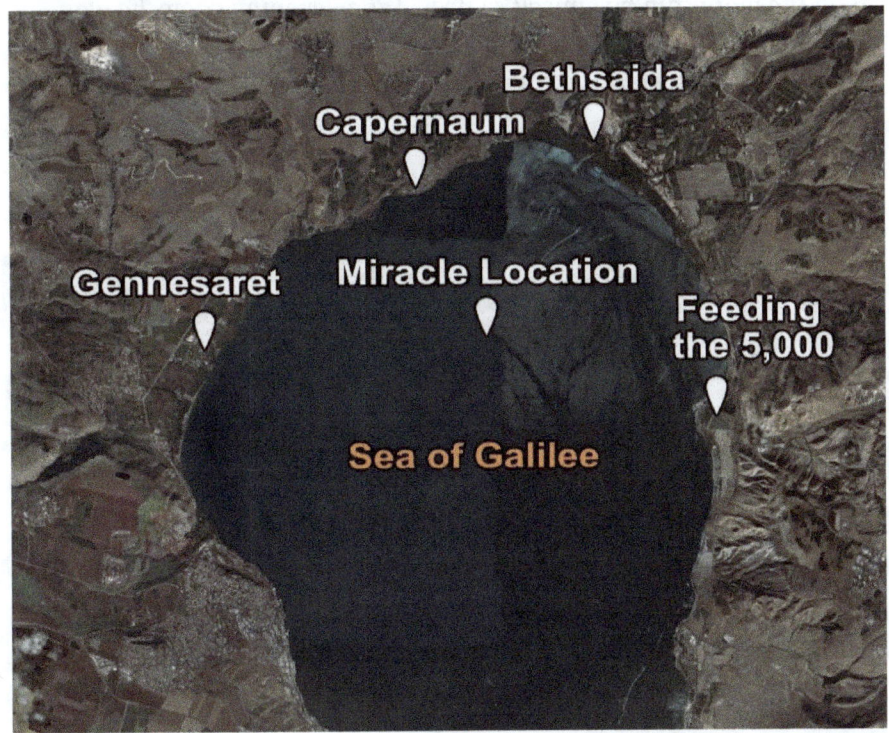

6. Place Jesus walked on water.
7. Gennesaret
8. Sea of Galilee

Jesus Walks on the Water and Calms the Sea in the Bible

1. **Immediately after feeding the 5,000, Jesus sent His disciples to the other side of the sea.**

    Matthew 14:22: *Immediately he made the disciples get into the boat and go before him to the other side, while he dismissed the crowds.*

    Mark 6:45: *Immediately he made his disciples get into the boat and go before him to the other side, to **Bethsaida**, while he dismissed the crowd.*

    John 6:16–17: *When evening came, his disciples went down to the sea, 17 got into a boat, and started across the sea to **Capernaum**.*

    The summary of these verses indicates that they were headed east to the other side of the sea.

2. **Jesus went up on a mountain to pray.**

    Matthew 14:23: *And after he had dismissed the crowds, he went up on the mountain by himself to pray. When evening came, he was there alone.*

3. **Jesus sends a strong storm.**

    Matthew 14:24: *But the boat by this time was a long way from the land, beaten by the waves, for the wind was against them.*

    Mark 6:48: *And he saw that they were making headway painfully, for the wind was against them.*

    John 6:17–18: *It was now dark, and Jesus had not yet come to them. 18 The sea became rough because a strong wind was blowing.*

4. **Jesus came to the disciples walking on the sea.**

   Matthew 14:25: *And in the fourth watch of the night [3:00–6:00 am] he came to them, walking on the sea.*

   John 6:19: *When they had rowed about three or four miles, they saw Jesus walking on the sea and coming near the boat.*

5. **The disciples became terrified.**

   Matthew 14:26: *But when the disciples saw him walking on the sea, they were terrified, and said, "It is a ghost!" and they cried out in fear.*

6. **The emotional state of the disciples:**
   - They were already exhausted from their ministry of being sent out two by two.
   - They had a long day of ministry.
   - They rowed all night in a state of panic and desperation.
   - They missed a night of sleep.
   - It was still dark, so it was probably around 4:00 am.
   - They feared for their lives.
   - They were alone.
   - It was dark.
   - They were terrified when they saw Jesus walking on the sea.

7. **Jesus spoke to them.**

   Matthew 14:27: *But immediately Jesus spoke to them, saying, "Take heart; it is I [I AM, in Greek]. Do not be afraid."*

8. **Peter walked on water for a moment.**

   Matthew 14:28–31: *And Peter answered him, "Lord, if it is you, command me to come to you on the water." 29 He said, "Come." So Peter got out of the boat and walked on the water and came to Jesus. 30 But when he saw the wind, he was afraid, and beginning to sink* he cried out, "Lord, save me." 31 Jesus immediately reached out his hand and took hold of him, saying to him, "O you of little faith, why did you doubt?"

9. **The disciples worshiped Jesus as Lord and Messiah.**

    Matthew 14:32–33: *And when they got into the boat, the wind ceased. 33 And those in the boat **worshiped him**, saying, **"Truly you are the Son of God."***

    Mark 6:52: *And he got into the boat with them, and the wind ceased. And they were **utterly astounded**.*

    This miracle was a major turning point in the lives of the disciples. The deity of Jesus was now deeply embedded in their hearts and lives, and they would never be the same.

10. **Jesus and the disciples miraculously arrived at the other side of the sea at Gennesaret.**

    John 6:21: *Then they were glad to take him into the boat, and **immediately** the boat was at the land to which they were going.*

11. **After already being exhausted and missing a night of sleep, they had more ministry awaiting them.**

    Matthew 14:34–36: *And when they had crossed over, they came to land at **Gennesaret**. 35 And when the men of that place recognized him, they sent around to all that region and brought to him all who were sick 36 and implored him that they might only touch the fringe of his garment. And as many as touched it were made well.*

Gennesaret boat dock

Faith Lesson from Jesus Walking on Water and Calming the Sea

1. Jesus embedded in the lives of His disciples that He was God. Do we believe in the deity of Christ and that He was God in the flesh?
2. Like Peter and the disciples, are we of little faith sometimes?
3. Like the disciples, we, too, are often surrounded by serious problems. Do we realize Jesus cares for us during the storms in

our lives?

4. Like the disciples, we can often feel tired and alone in our trials and problems. Do we understand we are not alone, and God is caring for us?

5. Peter walked on the water a moment and then took his eyes off Jesus and focused on the storm. Therefore, he sank into the water. Do we understand that in order to navigate the storms in our lives, we must keep our eyes on Jesus despite the raging problems around us?

6. Jesus was the one who sent the storm in order to teach His disciples who He was and their need for faith in Him. Do we understand that Jesus also sends storms to teach us the same truths?

7. Jesus and the disciples often had long days of exhausting ministry. Are we willing to do the same?

Journal/Notes:

Kursi

Location

1. Kursi is the place where two demon-possessed men were healed.
2. The demons who lived in these men were cast into a herd of pigs that ran down a steep bank into the sea.
3. It took place on the east side of the Sea of Galilee in the region of the Gerasenes or Gadarenes. This place was also called Kurshi in Hebrew and Kursy in Arabic.

4. It was in the region of the Decapolis.
5. The Decapolis was made up of 10 Roman cities that functioned like city-states. It was a region outside of Jewish authority and inhabited by Jews and Gentiles.
6. It was an immoral area that represented all that sinful humanity had to offer. Therefore, it was considered unclean to the Jews.
7. The caves where the demon-possessed men lived can be seen on the hillside above Kursi.
8. Today, this site contains the ruins of the largest Byzantine monastery complex in Israel. It dates from the middle of the 5th century and was built to commemorate what took place here.

Historical Background

1. Jesus and His disciples were coming from the Capernaum area, where Jesus had just performed many miracles and preached about the Parables of the Kingdom.
2. On the boat ride to this area, Jesus performed an astounding miracle of calming the sea and storm.

   Matthew 8:23–27: *And when he got into the boat, his disciples followed him. 24 And behold, there arose a great storm on the sea, so*

Sea of Galilee Sites

that the boat was being swamped by the waves; but he was asleep. 25 And they went and woke him, saying, "Save us, Lord; we are perishing." 26 And he said to them, "Why are you afraid, O you of little faith?" Then he rose and rebuked the winds and the sea, and there was a great calm. 27 And the men marveled, saying, "What sort of man is this, that even winds and sea obey him?"

3. This event is the most detailed account of an exorcism (casting out demons) in the Bible.

Places of Interest

1. Capernaum
2. Calming the Storm and Sea
3. Byzantine Monastery Complex
4. Tombs above Kursi
5. Beach where Jesus and His disciples arrived.
6. Steep hill the pigs ran down into the sea.
7. Decapolis Area

Kursi in the Bible

1. **When Jesus and His disciples arrived at the country of the Gadarenes, they were greeted by two demon-possessed men.**

   Matthew 8:28-29: *And when he came to the other side, to the country of the Gadarenes, two demon-possessed men met him, coming out of the tombs, so fierce that no one could pass that way. 29 And behold, they cried out, "What have you to do with us, O Son of God? Have you come here to torment us before the time?"*

2. **In the account of this story in Mark, it focuses on one of the demon-possessed men.**

   Mark 5:1-2: *They came to the other side of the sea, to the country of the Gerasenes. 2 And when Jesus had stepped out of the boat, immediately there met him out of the tombs a man with an unclean spirit.*

3. **The life of this demon-possessed man was a nightmarish living hell.**

   Mark 5:3-5: *He lived among the tombs. And no one could bind him anymore, not even with a chain, 4 for he had often been bound with shackles and chains, but he wrenched the chains apart, and he broke the shackles in pieces. No one had the strength to subdue him. 5 Night and day among the tombs and on the mountains he was always crying out and cutting himself with stones.*

4. **The legion of demons indwelling this man recognized who Jesus was.**

   Mark 5:6-9: *And when he saw Jesus from afar, he ran and fell down before him. 7 And crying out with a loud voice, he said, "What have you to do with me, Jesus, Son of the Most High God? I adjure you by God, do not torment me." 8 For he was saying to him, "Come out of the man, you unclean spirit!" 9 And Jesus asked him, "What is your name?" He replied, "My name is Legion [5,000 demons], for we are many."*

Sea of Galilee Sites

5. **Jesus cast this legion of demons into a herd of pigs who ran into the sea.**

   Mark 5:10–13: *And he begged him earnestly not to send them out of the country. 11 Now a great herd of pigs was feeding there on the hillside, 12 and they begged him, saying, "Send us to the pigs; let us enter them." 13 So he gave them permission. And the unclean spirits came out, and entered the pigs, and the herd, numbering about two thousand, rushed down the steep bank into the sea and were drowned in the sea.*

6. **The demon-possessed man was healed, and news spread rapidly to the whole region.**

   Mark 5:14–17: *The herdsmen fled and told it in the city and in the country. And people came to see what it was that had happened. 15 And they came to Jesus and saw the demon-possessed man, the one who had had the legion, sitting there, clothed and*  *in his right mind, and they were afraid. 16 And those who had seen it described to them what had happened to the demon-possessed man and to the pigs. 17 And they began to beg Jesus to depart from their region.*

7. **Jesus sent the healed man into the Decapolis region to tell them the great things God had done for him.**

   Mark 5:18–20: *As he was getting into the boat, the man who had been possessed with demons begged him that he might be with him. 19 And he did not permit him but said to him, "Go home to your friends and tell them how much the Lord has done for you, and how he has had mercy on you." 20 And he went away and began to proclaim in the Decapolis how much Jesus had done for him, and everyone marveled.*

Faith Lesson from Kursi

1. The demon-possessed man was in deep bondage and torment from the host of demons who lived within him. Do we believe demonic possession and oppression are a reality?
2. Jesus showed His power over the demonic realm by casting the legion of demons into a herd of 2,000 pigs. Do we believe Christ is Lord over Satan and all demonic rulers and principalities in the universe?

Tombs above Kursi

3. Jesus told the demon-possessed man to go and tell others how much the Lord had done for him.
4. History records that as a result of this man's obedience, a large community of believers was established in this area and had great influence on the early church for many centuries.
5. One of our best tools in sharing the gospel is just to tell others what God has done for us. Have we carefully defined our testimony, and are we committed to using it in sharing Christ with others?

Journal/Notes:

Sea of Galilee Sites

Magdala: Mary Magdalene

Location

1. Magdala, also known as Migdal, is located on the northwestern shore of the Sea of Galilee.
2. It was located on the Via Maris (International Highway linking Africa with Asia and Europe).

Historical Background

1. This particular part of Magdala was recently discovered in 2009. It's believed a flash flood covered it sometime in the latter part of the 1st century as there have been no coins or artifacts found dating later than 67 AD.
2. It was a fishing village and had one of the largest fish markets in the northern Galilee area.
3. It has one of the oldest, well-preserved synagogues in Israel.
4. This synagogue was in use during the time of Jesus, and He certainly would have preached here regularly.

   Matthew 4:23: *And he went throughout all Galilee, teaching in their synagogues and proclaiming the gospel of the kingdom and healing every disease and every affliction among the people.*

5. On one occasion, Jesus came to this area after feeding 4,000 people on the eastern side of the Sea of Galilee.

   Matthew 15:38–39: *Those who ate were four thousand men, besides women and children. 39 And after sending away the crowds, he got into the boat and went to the region of Magadan (Magdala).*

6. It had a population of around 1,000–2,000 people during the time of Christ.
7. It had a boat harbor.
8. It has a rare stone replica of the temple in Jerusalem with detailed carvings showing different aspects of the temple.

Sea of Galilee & Northern Biblical Sites Guide

9. Magdala was the hometown of the famous Jewish historian Josephus.
10. It was the hometown of Mary Magdalene, from whom Christ cast out 7 demons.

Places of Interest

1. Synagogue
2. Beth Midrash (teaching area in the synagogue).
3. Stone with grooves (used for reading the scrolls in the synagogue).
4. A rare stone replica of the temple in Jerusalem in the synagogue.
5. Well preserved mosaics in the synagogue.
6. Scroll storage room in the synagogue.
7. Marketplace
8. Fish Market Area
9. Residential Area
10. Mikvahs
11. Harbor

Sea of Galilee Sites

12. Byzantine Monastery
13. Duc In Altum (Latin for "Put out into the deep") is a spiritual center in Magdala where all can worship. It has a unique Galilean boat as an altar and has a beautiful view behind it of the Sea of Galilee. This center was built in honor of Mary Magdalene. One of its purposes is to honor and support women today.

Magdala (Mary Magdalene) in the Bible

1. **Jesus preached here regularly.**

   Matthew 4:23: *And he went throughout all Galilee, teaching in their synagogues and proclaiming the gospel of the kingdom and healing every disease and every affliction among the people.*

   Matthew 15:38–39: *Those who ate were four thousand men, besides women and children. 39 And after sending away the crowds, he got into the boat and went to the region of* **Magadan** *(Magdala).*

2. **Jesus cast out 7 demons from Mary Magdalene.**

   Luke 8:1–3: *Soon afterward he went on through cities and villages, proclaiming and bringing the good news of the kingdom of God. And the twelve were with him, 2 and also some women who had been healed of evil spirits and infirmities:* **Mary, called Magdalene**, *from whom seven demons had gone out, 3 and Joanna, the wife of Chuza, Herod's household manager, and Susanna, and many others, who provided for them out of their means.*

3. **Mary was likely a wealthy widow as she followed Christ everywhere and supported the ministry of Jesus financially.**

4. **A strong case could be made that Mary was one of Christ's most devoted and loyal followers.**

   She followed Jesus everywhere and supported Him financially, she was present at the mock trial of Jesus, she heard Pontius Pilate pronounce the death sentence upon Jesus, she saw Jesus beaten and humiliated by the crowd, she was one of the women who stood near Jesus during the crucifixion to try to comfort Him, and she was the first woman Christ appeared to after rising from the dead.

5. **Mary looked from a distance at Christ's crucifixion and then moved in closer during His last suffering hours on the Cross.**

   Mark 15:40: *There were also women looking on from a distance, among whom were **Mary Magdalene**, and Mary the mother of James the younger and of Joses, and Salome.*

   John 19:25: *But standing by the cross of Jesus were his mother and his mother's sister, Mary the wife of Clopas, and **Mary Magdalene**.*

6. **Mary Magdalene helped buy expensive spices to anoint the body of Jesus after His crucifixion.**

   Mark 16:1: *When the Sabbath was over, **Mary Magdalene**, Mary the mother of James, and Salome bought spices so that they might go to anoint Jesus' body.*

7. **Mary was the earliest witness to the resurrection of Jesus and was sent by Jesus to tell the others.**

   Mark 16:9: *When Jesus rose early on the first day of the week, **he appeared first to Mary Magdalene**, out of whom he had driven seven demons.*

   John 20:11–18: *But **Mary** stood weeping outside the tomb, and as she wept, she stooped to look into the tomb. 12 And she saw two angels in white, sitting where the body of Jesus had lain, one at the head and one at the feet. 13 They said to her, "Woman, why are you weeping?" She said to them, "They have taken away my Lord, and I do not know where they have laid him." 14 Having said this, she turned around and saw Jesus standing, but she did not know that it was Jesus. 15 Jesus said to her, "Woman, why are you weeping? Whom are you seeking?" Supposing him to be the gardener, she said to him, "Sir, if you have carried him away, tell me*

Synagogue

where you have laid him, and I will take him away." 16 Jesus said to her, "Mary." She turned and said to him in Aramaic, "Rabboni!" (which means Teacher). 17 Jesus said to her, "Do not cling to me, for I have not yet ascended to the Father; but go to my brothers and say to them, 'I am ascending to my Father and your Father, to my God and your God.'" 18 **Mary Magdalene** *went and announced to the disciples, "I have seen the Lord"—and that he had said these things to her.*

8. **Even at the very end, Mary never lost her first love for Jesus.**

    Revelation 2:4: *But I have this against you, that you have left your first love.*

9. **There is also no doubt Mary served Christ alongside the apostles the rest of her life.**

Faith Lesson from Magdala and Mary Magdalene

1. Christ cast out 7 demons from Mary. This changed her life forever and filled her with deep gratitude to Jesus. Are we grateful for what God has done for us as well?
2. Mary loved Christ profoundly and was one of His most devoted followers. She is the model of what it means to love the Lord your God with all your heart, soul, mind, and strength. Are we devoted to Christ as Mary was?
3. Mary supported Jesus' ministry financially. Do we support the ministries of Jesus as well?
4. Mary never lost her first love for Christ. Have we lost our first love?

Journal/Notes:

Mount Arbel

Location

1. Mount Arbel is located on the west side of the Sea of Galilee and is the tallest mountain around the sea.
2. It has a spectacular view of the Sea of Galilee.
3. It rises about 1,200 ft. (365 m.) above the Sea of Galilee.
4. It has on its eastern side a cliff that drops right down to the Sea of Galilee basin.
5. This cliff has many natural caves that have been used throughout history for battles and protection purposes.

Historical Background

1. History and tradition locate Mount Arbel as the place where Christ gave the Great Commission mandate to go into all the world and preach the gospel.
2. Many theologians believe this is the place because it is the tallest mountain in the area and provides a perfect view of the Sea of Galilee.
3. Because Christ spent around 50–70% of His ministry time around the Sea of Galilee, Mount Arbel would have provided the perfect backdrop when Christ gave the powerful Great Commission mandate to His disciples. From this location, we can easily see:
   - Magdala
   - The area where Christ likely called several of His disciples.
   - Chorazin
   - Tabgha
   - Capernaum
   - Bethsaida

Sea of Galilee Sites

- Kursi
  - Where Jesus walked on water and calmed the sea.
4. The Great Commission was one of the last contacts Christ had with His disciples, which shows the importance of this commandment.
5. The cliffs of Mount Arbel have natural caves that have been used as shelters for rebels against Herod the Great, revolts against the Romans, and again in later periods. There are ruins of Hellenistic, Roman, and Byzantine villages that lie below the cliffs and on its southwestern side.

Places of Interest

1. Park Entrance
2. Lookout Location
3. Arbel Cliffs
4. Magdala
5. Sea of Galilee
6. Hellenistic, Roman, and Byzantine villages that lie below the cliffs.
7. Ancient Synagogue
8. Fortress
9. Hiking Trail

Mount Arbel in the Bible

1. **Mount Arbel is the believed place where Christ gave the Great Commission.**

   Matthew 28:16–20: *Now the eleven disciples went to **Galilee, to the mountain** to which Jesus had directed them. 17 And when they saw him, they worshiped him, but some doubted. 18 And Jesus came and said to them, "All authority in heaven and on earth has been given to me. 19 Go therefore and make disciples of all nations, baptizing them in the name of the Father and of the Son and of the Holy Spirit, 20 teaching them to observe all that I have commanded you. And behold, I am with you always, to the end of the age."*

2. **What does the phrase "All authority in heaven and on earth has been given to me" mean?**

   Colossians 1:15–17: *He [Christ] is the image of the invisible God, the firstborn of all creation. 16 For by him all things were created, in heaven and on earth, visible and invisible, whether thrones or dominions or rulers or authorities—all things were created through him and for him. 17 And he is before all things, and in him all things hold together.*

   - Christ is the image of the invisible God. He is God in the flesh so we can understand and know Him better.
   - Christ created all things in heaven and on earth.
   - He created all thrones, dominions, rulers, and authorities, and rules over them.
   - He is the head of all things.
   - All creation is held together and sustained by His power.

3. **During Christ's ministry on earth, He performed every class of miracle to show He was Lord of every aspect of creation.**

- Sickness – Christ healed every kind of sickness among countless people.
- Demons and the demonic world – Christ repeatedly cast out demons from many people.
- Weather – Christ calmed the sea and storms.
- Nature – Christ cursed a fig tree, and it died.
- Animals – Christ cast out demons into a herd of swine, He performed the miraculous catches of fish, and He rode into Jerusalem on an untamed donkey.

Caves and fortress on the cliffs of Mt. Arbel

- Food – Christ fed 5,000 and 4,000 people.
- The authority to forgive sins – Only God has this authority, so Christ showed Himself as being fully God.
- Death – Christ raised numerous people from the dead, and He Himself rose from the dead.

4. **Every knee in heaven and earth will bow before the authority of Christ.**

   Philippians 2:9–11: *Therefore God has highly exalted him and bestowed on him the name that is above every name, 10 so that at the name of Jesus every knee should bow, in heaven and on earth and under the earth, 11 and every tongue confess that Jesus Christ is Lord, to the glory of God the Father.*

5. **Based upon the authority that Christ possesses, He commands us to go and make disciples.**

   Matthew 28:19–20: ***Go therefore*** *and make disciples of all nations, baptizing them in the name of the Father and of the Son and of the Holy Spirit, 20 teaching them to observe all that I have commanded you.*

Faith Lesson from Mount Arbel

1. All authority in heaven and earth has been given to Christ. Do we truly believe this?
2. We are all called to be missionaries.

    Acts 1:8: *But you will receive power when the Holy Spirit has come upon you, and you will be my witnesses in Jerusalem and in all Judea and Samaria, and to the end of the earth.*

3. Missionary means "One Sent."
4. Most missionary work is done on the local level in our own Jerusalem, as most are not called to foreign missions.

5. Just because we are not foreign missionaries does not mean we aren't a missionary at our local level.
6. Making disciples entails evangelizing.
7. To support foreign missions, there are a few ways we can be involved:
    - We can be goers.
    - We can be supporters by helping financially.
    - We can be encouragers to those in the field.
    - We can be helpers when missionaries return from the field and need help back home.
    - We can be prayer supporters.
    - Am I involved in foreign missions in at least one of the above ways?
8. In fulfilling the Great Commission, it's not just enough to be a good person and hope our life will show others we're different. We are commanded to go and speak!

Sea of Galilee Sites

9. While baptism does not save us, we are to emphasize it and baptize in the name of the Father, Son, and Holy Spirit. Have I been baptized, and do I encourage others to be baptized as well?
10. We are to teach others to obey all Christ has commanded. Am I involved in doing this?
11. We have the promise that the one who has all authority in heaven and on earth will be with us as we go to evangelize and make disciples. We should realize that:

    Mt. Arbel and the Sea of Galilee in the background

    - We are not alone in fulfilling the Great Commission but have Christ present and supernaturally helping us.
    - We have all the power and authority necessary in Christ, our helper, so we don't need to fear any demonic or contrary force.
12. Do I realize Christ is with me in every aspect as I strive to fulfill the Great Commission?

Journal/Notes:

Mount of Beatitudes

Location

1. The Mount of Beatitudes is located on a hill overlooking the northern shore of the Sea of Galilee.
2. It has a spectacular view of the sea.
3. It has great acoustics.

Historical Background

1. This sermon is the most complete and famous teaching Christ preached.
2. It's 3 chapters long and is found in Matthew 5-7.

3. In the same way the Law was given on Mount Sinai, many theologians see the Sermon on the Mount as the summary of the New Covenant.
4. In this sermon, Christ clarifies many Old Testament meanings and misinterpretations by constantly saying, *"You have heard it said, but I say to you."*
5. The view from the Sermon on the Mount is spectacular and provided a perfect backdrop for Christ's hearers to see as they contemplated His powerful message.
6. It was no accident that Christ chose this setting as He used nature and creation to aid in much of His teachings.
7. A Byzantine church was erected here in the 4th century and was used until the 7th century. Its ruins have been discovered just a little downhill from the present church here today.
8. Today, the Church of the Beatitudes is an octagonal building located on this site. It was built in 1938 for a Franciscan order of nuns. The eight sides of the church represent the eight beatitudes shown in Latin in the upper windows.

Sea of Galilee Sites

Places of Interest

1. Entrance
2. Mount of Beatitudes
3. Sea of Galilee
4. Church of the Beatitudes
5. Beatitude Monastery

The Sermon on the Mount in the Bible

1. **In the 8 beatitudes, everything is flipped or reversed from what most would understand as blessings.**

   Matthew 5:1–12: *Seeing the crowds, he went up on the mountain, and when he sat down, his disciples came to him. 2 And he opened his mouth and taught them, saying: 3 "Blessed are the poor in spirit, for theirs is the kingdom of heaven. 4 Blessed are those who mourn, for they shall be comforted. 5 Blessed are the meek, for they shall inherit the earth. 6 Blessed are those who hunger and thirst for righteousness, for they shall be satisfied. 7 Blessed are the merciful, for they shall receive mercy. 8 Blessed are the pure in heart, for they shall see God. 9 Blessed are the peacemakers, for they shall be called sons of God. 10 Blessed are those who are persecuted for righteousness' sake, for theirs is the kingdom of heaven. 11 Blessed* are you when others revile you and persecute you and utter all kinds of evil against you falsely on my account. 12 Rejoice and be glad, for your reward is great in heaven, for so they persecuted the prophets who were before you."

2. **Christ addressed the true essence of anger, adultery, divorce, keeping our word, how to treat our enemies, giving, prayer, and what genuine salvation looks like.**
3. **He taught about storing our riches in heaven and how to handle worry and stress.**

Matthew 6:19–21: *Do not lay up for yourselves treasures on earth, where moth and rust destroy and where thieves break in and steal, 20 but lay up for yourselves treasures in heaven, where neither moth nor rust destroys and where thieves do not break in and steal. 21 For where your treasure is, there your heart will be also.*

Matthew 6:25–34: *Therefore, I tell you, do not be anxious about your life, what you will eat or what you will drink, nor about your body, what you will put on. Is not life more than food, and the body more than clothing? 26 Look at the birds of the air: they neither sow nor reap nor gather into barns, and yet your heavenly Father feeds them. Are you not of more value than they? 27 And which of you by being*

Mount of Beatitudes

anxious can add a single hour to his span of life? 28 And why are you anxious about clothing? Consider the lilies of the field, how they grow: they neither toil nor spin, 29 yet I tell you, even Solomon in all his glory was not arrayed like one of these. 30 But if God so clothes the grass of the field, which today is alive and tomorrow is thrown into the oven, will he not much more clothe you, O you of little faith? 31 Therefore do not be anxious, saying, "What shall we eat?" or "What shall we drink?" or "What shall we wear?" 32 For the Gentiles [nonbelievers] seek after all these things, and your heavenly Father *knows that you need them all. 33 **But seek first the kingdom of God and his righteousness, and all these things will be added to you.** 34 Therefore do not be anxious about tomorrow, for tomorrow will be anxious for itself. Sufficient for the day is its own trouble.*

4. **Christ ended His message with a sober warning about the importance of obeying and living out His words, not just listening to them.**

   Matthew 7:24–29: *Everyone then who hears these words of mine and does them will be like a wise man who built his house on the rock. 25 And the rain fell, and the floods came, and the winds blew and beat on that house, but it did not fall, because it had been founded on the rock. 26 And everyone who hears these words of mine and does not do them will be like a foolish man who built his house on the sand. 27 And the rain fell, and the floods came, and the winds blew and beat against that house, and it fell, and great was the fall of it. 28 And when Jesus finished these sayings, the crowds were astonished at his teaching, 29 for he was teaching them as one who had authority, and not as their scribes.*

Sea of Galilee from the Mount of Beatitudes

Faith Lesson from the Sermon on the Mount

1. Christ began His sermon by clarifying the principles of true blessings in life. Do we understand each principle, and are we living them out?
2. Christ focused on the heart attitude behind His commands. Do we understand that Christ looks at our hearts and motives for why we obey or don't obey His commands?
3. Christ stressed the importance of storing our riches in heaven and living for eternity. Do we care about our treasures in heaven, or are we mainly just focused on this life and the treasures it has to

offer?

4. Christ defined a wise person as one who lived out what He taught. He defined a foolish person as one who heard but did not put into practice what He taught. Do we tend to know what to do but not actually live it out?

Church of the Beatitudes

5. Are we building our lives on the sand or on the rock?

Journal/Notes:

Sea of Galilee Sites

Sower's Cove: Parables of the Kingdom

Location

1. Sower's Cove is located between Capernaum and Tabgha on the northern shore of the Sea of Galilee.
2. It's a natural cove with outstanding acoustics.
3. When Christ preached the Parables of the Kingdom, He went out of His house in Capernaum and sat by the sea. Tradition and the natural location of Sower's Cove make it an excellent candidate for the place where Christ preached these parables found in Matthew 13.

Historical Background

1. A parable is a story that illustrates a truth by using an example from nature.
2. The parables tell what the Kingdom of Heaven is like.
3. The term "Kingdom of Heaven" and "Kingdom of God" are the same. Matthew's gospel uses the term "Kingdom of Heaven" as it was directed to more of a Jewish audience. The Jews had such a high reverence for God that they didn't use His name much. They even took out the vowels in Yahweh to show reverence. The other Gospels mainly use the term "Kingdom of God" in their accounts.
4. Part of the reason Christ spoke in parables was to fulfill prophecies regarding judgment on the Israelites because of their dull and hardened hearts (Isaiah 6:9–10).

    Matthew 13:13–17: *This is why I speak to them in parables, because seeing they do not see, and hearing they do not hear, nor do they understand. 14 Indeed, in their case the prophecy of Isaiah is fulfilled that says: "You will indeed hear but never understand, and you will indeed see but never perceive." 15 For this people's heart has grown dull, and with their ears they can barely hear, and their*

Sea of Galilee & Northern Biblical Sites Guide

eyes they have closed, lest they should see with their eyes and hear with their ears and understand with their heart and turn, and I would heal them. 16 But blessed are your eyes, for they see, and your ears, for they hear. 17 For truly, I say to you, many prophets and righteous people longed to see what you see, and did not see it, and to hear what you hear, and did not hear it.

Places of Interest

1. Sower's Cove
2. Capernaum
3. Northern Shore of the Sea of Galilee
4. Mount of Beatitudes
5. Bethsaida
6. Tabgha
7. Sea of Galilee

Sea of Galilee Sites

Parable of the Sower in the Bible

1. **Jesus went out by the Sea of Galilee and told many parables; one of them was the Parable of the Sower.**

   Matthew 13:1-9: That same day Jesus went out of the house and sat beside the sea. 2 And great crowds gathered about him, so that he got into a boat and sat down. And the whole crowd stood on the beach. 3 And he told them many things in parables, saying: "A sower went out to sow. 4 And as he sowed, some seeds fell along the path, and the birds came and devoured them. 5 Other seeds fell on rocky ground, where they did not have much soil, and immediately they sprang up, since they had no depth of soil, 6 but when the sun rose, they were scorched. And

   since they had no root, they withered away. 7 Other seeds fell among thorns, and the thorns grew up and choked them. 8 Other seeds fell on good soil and produced grain, some a hundredfold, some sixty, some thirty. 9 He who has ears, let him hear."

2. **Jesus used the natural elements of nature found right in this area as illustrations for this parable.**

3. **Christ explains the meaning of the Parable of the Sower.**

   Matthew 13:18-23: Hear then the parable of the sower: 19 When anyone hears the word of the kingdom and does not understand it, the evil one comes and snatches away what has been sown in his heart. This is what was sown along the path. 20 As for what was sown on rocky ground, this is the one who hears the word and immediately receives it with joy, 21 yet he has no root in himself, but endures for a while, and when tribulation or persecution arises on account of the word, immediately he falls away. 22 As for what was sown among thorns, this is the one who hears the word, but the cares of the world and the deceitfulness of riches choke the word, and it proves unfruitful. 23 As for what was sown on good soil, this is the one who hears the word and understands it. He indeed bears fruit and yields, in one case a hundredfold, in another sixty, and in another thirty.

Summary of the Meaning of the Parable of the Sower

1. The seed is the Word of God.
2. The different soils represent the different kinds of hearts people can have.
3. The one who snatches away the seed is the Devil.
4. The hard soil is a hard heart that hears but refuses to let God's Word enter. They are unsaved and under Satan's control.
5. The rocky soil represents those who hear God's Word but don't continue when hard times and persecution come.
6. The weedy soil represents people who allow the worries of life and the pursuit of wealth to choke out God's Word, so they wither up and die.
7. The last soil that produces a harvest represents true believers who persevere in their faith, and in so doing, produce fruit.

8. It seems clear that the first 3 kinds of soils represent unsaved people.
9. Only the last soil that produced fruit represents the truly saved person, as fruit is the example used throughout Scripture to refer to genuinely saved people.

Other Parables Christ Taught at Sower's Cove

1. Parable of the Weeds (Tares)

2. Parable of the Mustard Seed and the Leaven
3. Parable of the Hidden Treasure
4. Parable of the Pearl of Great Value
5. Parable of the Net

Faith Lesson from Sower's Cove

1. Part of the reason Christ spoke in parables was to fulfill prophecies regarding judgment on the Israelites because of their dull and unbelieving hearts. Are our hearts dull of hearing? What are we doing to protect our hearts from becoming dull of hearing?

2. What kind of soil (heart) do we possess? Is it hard? Is it stony, shallow, and pulls away from God when trials and suffering come? Is it full of the cares and distractions of this world? Or is it producing much fruit for God?
3. The good soil produced different amounts of fruit; some yielded a hundred-fold, some sixty-fold, and some thirty-fold. How much fruit are you producing for God?

Journal/Notes:

Tabgha

Location

1. Tabgha is located on the northwest side of the Sea of Galilee.
2. There are 7 springs found in this area which provided one of the best fishing places around the sea.
3. Some of the springs provided warm sulfuric water that caused the fish to gather here. It was also used for health purposes, and many came from far away to find healing and relief in its waters.
4. Waters from these springs were also taken to nearby fields and villages via canals.
5. This site is the traditional place where it's believed Christ fed the 5,000. The modern Church of the Multiplication stands on the site of a 4th-century church that has undergone several renovations throughout the centuries. In 1982 the church that was here was replaced by the modern Church of the Multiplication.
6. However, we don't believe Tabgha is the biblical place for the feeding of the 5,000 for the following reasons:
    - Scripture says Jesus and His disciples were headed to Bethsaida to a desolate place (Mark 6:31; Luke 9:10). Tabgha is in a very populated area and on the opposite side of the sea from Bethsaida, which was on the eastern side of the sea.
    - The large population area was from Tiberias to Capernaum (the northwestern side). The deserted area was on the northeastern side of the sea in the Bethsaida region.
    - Bethsaida was a fishing village on the northeastern side of the sea.
    - Immediately after feeding the 5,000, Jesus ordered His disciples to cross over to the other side of the sea (Matt. 14:22).

- While the disciples were crossing over to the other side is when a strong storm arose. Jesus walked on water (Peter attempted to as well), and Jesus calmed the storm.
- The storm seems to have changed the course of their destination as Scripture says that they ended up arriving in the area of Gennesaret (Matt. 14:34–36).
- Gennesaret is located on the northwestern side of the sea where all the population is.
- Gennesaret is less than 2 miles (3 km.) south of Tabgha. If the miracle happened at Tabgha, going from Tabgha to Gennesaret wouldn't be crossing over the other side of the sea as both towns are nearby to each other.

Tabgha

- After Christ arrived at Gennesaret, many heard he had arrived, and a large multitude gathered for healing. If Christ had just been in the area of Tabgha, it wouldn't make sense that a large crowd would gather again right after Christ had just been there.
- For these reasons, we believe the best biblical location for the feeding of the 5,000 is just south of Bethsaida in an open flat area. It seems to fit the text and the geography of the land best.

7. Even though Tabgha might not be the location of the feeding of the 5,000, it's a great place to reflect and commemorate this miracle. The important thing is that the miracle really happened, not that we get the place exactly right.
8. It's also the site where it's believed Christ restored Peter after His resurrection. The Church of the Primacy of St. Peter marks the place where this event took place. The church today was built in 1933 and incorporated parts of an earlier 4th-century church. A building made of black basalt was built in 1934 and

commemorates this place.
9. The restoration of Peter will be our focus at this site.

Historical Background

1. The disciples had returned to their hometowns on the northern shore of the Sea of Galilee after the death, burial, and resurrection of Christ in Jerusalem.
2. They undoubtedly felt very depressed, lonely, and as if their whole world had come to an end.
3. Their beloved Master had been crucified, and they were left wondering what would happen now.

Church of the Multiplication

4. They probably called into question how they had spent their past 3 ½ years following Christ.
5. Peter especially felt depressed and spiritually sick. His last contact with Christ was that of hearing the cock crow in declaration to the fact that he had just denied his Lord and Master 3 times after he had just moments earlier said he would follow Him even to death.

Places of Interest

1. Church of the Multiplication
2. Stone inside the Church of the Multiplication upon which tradition holds that Christ multiplied the fish and bread.
3. Church of the Primacy of St. Peter
4. Stone inside the Church of the Primacy of St. Peter upon which tradition holds that Christ fed the disciples after His resurrection, and where Christ restored Peter.
5. Beach nearby to the Church of the Primacy of St. Peter.
6. Heart-shaped stones by the beach.
7. Rock Monument with a carved cross and verse.
8. Mount of Beatitudes

Restoration of Peter in the Bible

1. **After Christ's crucifixion and resurrection, the disciples went back to fishing like old times.**

   John 21:1–3: *Afterward Jesus appeared again to his disciples, by the Sea of Tiberius. It happened this way: 2 Simon Peter, Thomas (called Didymus), Nathanael from Cana in Galilee, the sons of Zebedee, and two other disciples were together [8 disciples in all]. 3 "I'm going out to fish," Simon Peter told them, and they said, "We'll go with you." So they went out and got into the boat, but that night they caught nothing.*

2. **Jesus appears to the disciples.**

   John 21:4–14: *Early in the morning, Jesus stood on the shore, but the disciples did not realize that it was Jesus. 5 He called out to them, "Friends, haven't you any fish?" "No," they answered. 6 He said, "Throw your net on the right side of the boat, and you will find some." When they did, they were unable to haul the net in because of the large number of fish. 7 Then the disciple whom Jesus loved said to Peter, "It is the Lord!" As soon as Simon Peter heard him say, "It is the Lord," he wrapped his outer garment around him (for he had taken it off) and jumped into the water. 8 The other disciples followed in the boat, towing the net full of fish, for they were not far from shore, about a hundred yards. 9 When they landed, they saw a* fire of burning coals there with fish on it, and some bread [in John 18:18 Peter denied Christ by a charcoal fire]. 10 Jesus said to them, "Bring some of the fish you have just caught." 11 Simon Peter climbed aboard and dragged the net ashore. It was full of large fish, 153 [according to Hebrew alphabetics, this number meant "I Am God"], but even with so many, the net was not torn. 12 Jesus said to them, "Come and have breakfast." None of the disciples dared ask him, "Who are you?" They knew it was the Lord. 13 Jesus came, took the bread and gave it to them, and did the same with the fish [same food as the feeding of the 5,000]. 14 This was now the third time Jesus appeared to his disciples after he was raised from the dead.

3. **Jesus restores Peter.**

John 21:15–17: *When they had finished eating, Jesus said to Simon Peter, "Simon son of John, do you truly love me more than these?" "Yes, Lord," he said, "you know that I love you." Jesus said, "Feed my lambs." 16 Again Jesus said, "Simon son of John, do you truly love me?"*

Church of the Primacy of St. Peter

He answered, "Yes, Lord, you know that I love you." Jesus said, "Take care of my sheep." 17 The third time he said to him, "Simon son of John, do you love me?" Peter was hurt because Jesus asked him the third time, "Do you love me?" He said, "Lord, you know all things; you know that I love you." Jesus said, "Feed my sheep."

4. **This encounter was similar to the first time Christ called Peter to be His disciple.**

Luke 5:1–11: *On one occasion, while the crowd was pressing in on him to hear the word of God, he was standing by the lake of Gennesaret, 2 and he saw two boats by the lake, but the fishermen had gone out of them and were washing their nets. 3 Getting into one of the boats, which was Simon's, he asked him to put out a little from the land. And he sat down and taught the people from the boat.*

4 And when he had finished speaking, he said to Simon, "Put out into the deep and let down your nets for a catch." 5 And Simon answered, "Master, we toiled all night and took nothing! But at your word, I will let down the nets." 6 And when they had done this, they enclosed a large number of fish, and their nets were breaking. 7 They signaled to their partners in the other boat to come and help them. And they came and filled both the boats, so that they began to sink. 8 But when Simon Peter saw it, he fell down at Jesus' knees, saying, "Depart from me, for I am a sinful man, O Lord." 9 For he and all who were with him were astonished at the catch of fish that they had taken, 10 and so also were James and John, sons of Zebedee, who were partners with Simon. And Jesus said to Simon, "Do not be afraid; from now on you will be catching men." 11 And when they had brought their boats to land, they left everything and followed him.

Faith Lesson from Tabgha

1. Peter's original calling to be a disciple and his restoration follow the same miracle pattern. Christ did this on purpose because He wanted Peter to remember his roots and beginning.
2. Christ was the one who reached out to Peter and took the initiative to restore him.
3. Jesus asked Peter if he loved Him 3 times because Peter denied Him 3 times.
4. God realizes we are human and make mistakes.
5. The main thing God looks for in restoration is a spirit of repentance and a contrite, humble heart.
6. Am I in need of restoration in some way?
7. Do I understand that God is more interested in my restoration with Him than I probably am?

Journal/Notes:

Yardenit Baptismal Site

Location

There are two main baptismal sites on the Jordan River.

Yardenit Baptismal Site

1. Yardenit is just a couple hundred yards (meters) west of Hwy. 90, at the southern tip of the Sea of Galilee.
2. It's a popular spot, and the water is clean and abundant.
3. For those desiring to get baptized here in the Jordan River, the Yardenit gift shop provides white robes and towels for a small fee.
4. Yardenit has a large gift shop for the purchase of souvenirs and other miscellaneous items as well.
5. Yardenit is also a great place to view the Jordan River.
6. Entrance to the site is free.

Jordan River Baptismal Site of Jesus (Qasr al-Yahud)

1. This baptismal site is located about 2 miles (3.2 km.) east of Hwy. 90, across from Jericho.
2. It's also known as Qaser al-Yahud, Kasser al-Yahud, and the Baptismal Site of Jesus.
3. It's the place where it's believed Jesus was baptized and where John the Baptist and the disciples of Jesus baptized many people as well.
4. The water is not as clean as Yardenit, but thousands of pilgrims are baptized there each year because of its spiritual significance.
5. It's also the believed location where the Israelites crossed the Jordan River to enter the Promised Land.

   (For more, please see Jordan River Baptismal Site of Jesus.)

Sea of Galilee Sites

Places of Interest

1. Yardenit Baptismal Site
2. Jordan River
3. Parking Area
4. Hwy. 90
5. Sea of Galilee

Historical Background

1. The concept of baptism is rooted in the Old Testament. As far back as Genesis, eight people were saved from the great flood of God's judgment. The Apostle Peter indicated that the water of the flood "symbolizes baptism that now saves you" (1 Pet. 3:21).

2. Old Testament prophets such as Isaiah, Ezekiel, and King David likewise used water as an external symbol for internal cleansing (Isa. 1:16; Ezek. 36:25; Ps. 51:2).

    Isaiah 1:16: *Wash yourselves; make yourselves clean; remove the evil of your deeds from before my eyes; cease to do evil.*

3. The word baptize, baptized, baptizing, or baptismal is mentioned around 83 times in the New Testament and, therefore, shows the value God places on it.

(For the full Bible teaching on baptism, please see the Jordan River Baptismal Site of Jesus – Qsar al-Yahud Baptismal Site.)

Other Sites Around the Sea of Galilee

Beit Yigal Allon Centre, Ginosar: The Galilee Boat

The main attraction of Kibbutz Ginnosar is the ancient fishing boat, now known as the Sea of Galilee Boat, displayed here in the Beit Yigal Allon Museum. Discovered in 1986, buried near the edge of the lake in

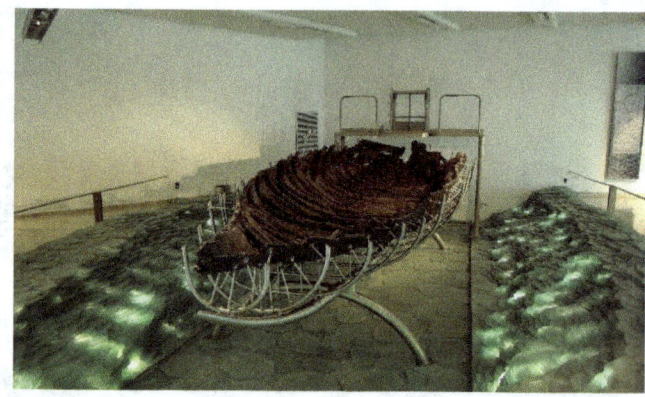

mud, the boat is dated somewhere between 70 BC and 90 AD, meaning that it could have been in use during the time of Jesus. The boat is made from cedar wood and is about 27 ft. (8.27 m.) long and 7.5 ft. (2.3 m.) wide. Although there is no proof that the boat could have been used by Jesus or one of his disciples, many people have nicknamed it the Jesus Boat.

Berko Archaeological Park

The Berko Archaeological Museum provides a unique glimpse into Tiberias of the first century. Tiberias was founded in 18 AD by Herod Antipas, son of Herod the Great and Jewish ruler of the Galilee (4 BC-39 AD). Herod Antipas made the new city his capital, and named the city after the Roman emperor, Tiberius Caesar. The park includes an ancient Roman gate, a theater, bathhouse, and a drainage system that is a thousand years old. It also contains gardens with paths throughout and balconies offering an overall view of the ancient city.

The Theater of Roman Tiberias was constructed in the 1st century AD, then enlarged in the 2nd or 3rd centuries AD, and had a seating capacity of 7,000 people. It continued to be used for gatherings until the end of the Byzantine period and was destroyed by an earthquake that struck the city in 749 AD.

The site is located near the southern entrance of Tiberias, between the ancient cemetery and the hotels of Hammat Tiberias. A parking lot is located near the south gate, north of the Holiday Inn hotel.

Gamla Nature Reserve

High in the Golan Heights of northern Israel stretches the Gamla Nature Reserve, which is home to the ancient city of Gamla, and the Gamla Stream Waterfall (the tallest flowing waterfall in Israel). The park is full of wildlife and breathtaking views.

Gamla (camel in Hebrew) was an ancient fortified city on the Golan Heights located on a high ridge above a crossing of two gorges. During the Great Revolt against the Romans in 66 AD, it became an important stronghold where Jewish rebels fought bravely until their fatal end. The observation terrace provides a

view from above the ancient city on its ridge and the remains of the early synagogue. To explore the ruins of Gamla up close, you need to take the hiking trail, aptly named "Ancient Trail," which is about .62 miles (1 km.) each way. However, because it involves some climbing and descending over stones, it can take about 2 hours. There is a viewing place by the park headquarters that grants a beautiful view of the ruins for those who don't care to hike down to them.

Gamla Stream Waterfall lookout point provides a view of the cliffs of the Gamla Stream canyon and a colony of nesting birds of prey. There is an easy 90-minute trail (45 minutes each way) leading to the lookout terrace from which the highest waterfall in Israel, 170 ft. (51 m.), flows year-round. Along the way, you will pass ancient dolmans and a collection of bronze age burial mounds made of huge boulders.

Hamat Tverya National Park

This park is in the ancient village of Hamat and is much older than Tiberias. "Hama" means hot spring. It was one of the fortified cities mentioned in the Bible within the Tribe of Naftali:

> "And the fortified cities were Tziddim, Tzer, and **Hamat**, and Rakkat, and Chinneret" (Josh. 19:35).

After the founding of Tiberias, Hamat became Hamat Tverya. The distance between the two cities was one mile (1.6 km.). In the park, the remains of mosaics from 3 different synagogues that were built one on top of the other, can be found. The first synagogue was built about 230 AD, the second existed in the 4th century AD, and the third was rebuilt after being destroyed in an earthquake in the 5th century. The synagogue underwent preservation, restoration, and reconstruction, and is now surrounded by glass walls.

Tiberias Hot Springs – Hamat Tverya National Park – On the Tiberias Hot Springs site, 17 thermo-mineral springs flow at a temperature of about 140 F (60 C). The water flows in a system of underground channels to the Turkish Hamam, a beautifully preserved 18th-century structure. Surplus water that does not flow into the Tiberias hot baths is collected in a pool located on-site. Because of the curative properties attributed to the waters, the Romans erected luxurious baths, attracting

people from all over the empire. The remains of the ancient Roman baths are located at the southern end of the site.

Hippos (Horvat Susita)

The ruins of the ancient city of Hippos (horse in Greek), known today as Horvat Susita, are located 1.2 miles (2 km.) east of the Sea of Galilee on the plateau of a diamond-shaped mountain, 1,148 ft. (350 m.) above the sea. The city was almost entirely isolated from its surroundings, with just a narrow saddle-bridge leading towards the western slopes of the Golan Heights. The entire city was surrounded by an imposing fortification wall.

The ruins of Hippos are of the Hellenistic, Roman, Byzantine, and Umayyad periods, dating back to the time between the 3rd century BC and 7th century AD. During the Roman period, Hippos belonged to the Decapolis, a group of ten cities that were regarded as centers of Greek culture in an area predominantly Jewish. Archaeologists have uncovered a main colonnaded street, Roman fortifications, public baths, and temples from both the Hellenistic and Roman periods. More recently, a Roman basilica and the remains of at least seven different churches built during the Byzantine period

have been uncovered. This confirms that by the 4th century AD, the majority of residents in the city were probably Christian. Hippos continued to exist until the mid-8th century, when the city was destroyed by the catastrophic earthquake of 749 AD and was never again resettled.

Mitzpe Ofir Observation Point

This is a beautiful lookout and rest area in the southern Golan Heights that offers a view of the entire Sea of Galilee. From this viewpoint, not only can you see the whole lake, but you can also see the Lower Galilee mountains, the Upper Galilee, and the Golan Heights. The lookout is also part of a long hiking trail down to old Derech Bnei Yehuda (village settlement). This is a great place to spend a late

afternoon and witness spectacular sunsets. Mitzpe Ofir was established and is maintained by Mr. Shaal of Givat Yoav, who chose this beautiful spot to memorialize his son Ofir, who died of a long illness when he was only 16 years old. A grove of 16 olive trees has been planted there, one for each year of Ofir's life.

Tiberias Promenade

The Yigal Allon Promenade in Tiberias is more commonly known as the Tiberias Promenade. It's located along the Sea of Galilee near the Old City of Tiberias and the small Marina. The Promenade offers a pleasant stroll by the water, allowing visitors to enjoy the beautiful view of the water, boats, and the marina.

You can take a ride on a boat on the Sea of Galilee from here as well. Sunset and the evening are exceptional times to visit the Promenade with its many restaurants and souvenir shops open and busy.

Tiberium Light Show

Israel's world-renowned multimedia design company created a breathtaking water-music-light show for Tiberias. This spectacular show features dancing fountains with artistic laser lights, music, and pyrotechnics screened onto jets of water, reaching over ten meters high to create a dazzling display of water and light. The show takes place at the south end of the Yigal Alon Promenade and is free to the public three times each evening from 7-9 pm, except in rainy weather. (Note: Tiberium depends on the water level of the Sea of Galilee. If the level is too high, the light show will not take place.)

Northern Israel Sites

Beth-Shean

Location

1. Beth-Shean, also known as Beit Shean or Bet She'an, was a major biblical and secular city for thousands of years.

2. It's located in the center of several main crossroads between the Jordan Valley and the Jezreel (Yizreel) Valley.
3. It's about 15 miles (25 km.) south of the southern tip of the Sea of Galilee and about 35 miles (55 km.) east of the Mediterranean Sea.
4. It's located on the Harod Stream, which provides it with much water. This Harod Stream is the same stream that originates at Harod Spring, just west of here about 15 miles, and is where Gideon chose 300 men under God's command to defeat the Midianites and other armies.
5. The main entrance faced the east, as did most other major cities and structures in ancient times. In fact, the word "orientation" comes from the word "orient," which means east. Because creation, the beginning civilizations, and the sun rose from the east, to be oriented was to position yourself focused on the east. Today, maps use the north for orientation, but in ancient days, maps used the east for orientation purposes.

Historical Background

1. Beth-Shean was a key city long before the arrival of the Israelites because of its location. In the late Canaanite period (1600–1400 BC), the Egyptians ruled the area and the entire land of Israel.
2. Later, around 1000 BC, the Philistines also ruled the city for a time as they hung the body of King Saul on its walls after defeating the armies of Israel in the Battle of Gilboa.

3. When King David reigned (1010–970 BC), he conquered Beth-Shean, which became part of Israel's territories.
4. Later, in 732 BC, the Assyrian king, Tiglath-Pileser III, destroyed Beth-Shean after defeating the northern Kingdom of Israel.
5. In the 4th century BC, Hellenistic (Greek) new settlers established a city-state (polis) in Beth-Shean. During the Hellenistic period, the city was named Nisa Scythopolis.
6. In 63 BC, the city was conquered by the Romans and became one of the cities of the Decapolis – a group of cities with a Hellenistic-Roman cultural character, most of them in Transjordan. Beth-Shean was one of the key cities of the Roman Empire in this area south of Galilee.
7. Beth-Shean was not far from Nazareth, so it's very likely when Jesus was young, he worked here with His father as a builder.
8. Undoubtedly Christ ministered here and walked by it regularly.
9. Beth-Shean was destroyed in 749 AD due to an enormous earthquake.
10. The biblical tel of Beth-Shean has around 20 layers of civilizations that have been discovered.

Places of Interest

1. Entrance
2. Old Testament Beth-Shean
3. Egyptian Governor's House
4. Tree marking the place where Saul's body was hanged.
5. Bathhouse – Often, it was a place of prostitution, so Christians avoided places like these.
6. Theater – Often, immoral and indecent acts took place there.

Therefore, early Christians avoided them and were persecuted as a result.

7. Cardo (Palladius Street) – Comes from the word "cardiac," which means the center street of the city.

8. Sigma – A mosaic depicting Tyche, Goddess of the city.
9. Pillars
10. Shopping Stores
11. Nymphaeum – Public Fountain
12. Marketplace (Agora) – Paul would be dragged into places like this (Acts 16:19).
13. Temple – Paul faced the gods of these temples in each Gentile city he ministered in (Acts 14:13).
14. Northern Street
15. Valley Street
16. Silvanus Street
17. Eastern Bathhouse
18. Public Bathrooms
19. Sacred Area
20. City Gate during Greek and Roman times.

Northern Israel Sites

Beth-Shean in the Bible

1. **Beth-Shean is mentioned in the division and conquering of the Promised Land.**

   Joshua 17:11: *Also, in Issachar and in Asher, Manasseh had **Beth-Shean** and its villages.*

2. **The Canaanites were a strong and fortified people.**

   Joshua 17:16: *The people of Joseph said, "The hill country is not enough for us. Yet all the Canaanites who dwell in the plain have chariots of iron, both those in **Beth-shean** and its villages and those in the Valley of Jezreel."*

3. **The tribe of Manasseh was not able to conquer the city of Beth-Shean and its villages.**

   Judges 1:27: *Manasseh did not drive out the inhabitants of **Beth-Shean** and its villages.*

4. **The major biblical event of Beth-Shean has to do with the life of King Saul.**

   Theater

   As a result of Saul's persistent disobedience and presuming upon God's grace, his life was taken by the Lord, and his body, along with his sons, were hanged here on the walls of the biblical Beth-Shean, which is the hill above the lower Beth-Shean.

Saul's Disobedient Life

1. **Saul had incredible jealousy and tried to kill David for many years.**

   Scripture records many times that Saul tried to kill David: 1 Samuel 18:11, 1 Samuel 18:25, 1 Samuel 19:9–15, 1 Samuel 20:31–33, 1 Samuel 23:9, and 1 Samuel 23:25–26. Saul even gave his daughter, Michal, in marriage to David as a means to ensnare and kill him.

2. **When Saul felt pressured during a battle, he offered sacrifices that only a priest was allowed to do.**

   1 Samuel 13:5–7: *And the Philistines mustered to fight with Israel, thirty thousand chariots and six thousand horsemen and troops like the sand on the seashore in multitude. They came up and encamped in Michmash, to the east of Beth-aven. 6 When the men of Israel saw that they were in trouble (for the people were hard pressed), the people hid themselves in caves and in holes and in rocks and in tombs and in cisterns, 7 and some Hebrews crossed the fords of the Jordan to the land of Gad and Gilead. Saul was still at Gilgal, and all the people followed him trembling.*

3. **Saul's unlawful sacrifice.**

   1 Samuel 13:8–14: *He waited seven days, the time appointed by Samuel. But Samuel did not come to Gilgal, and the people were scattering from him. 9 So Saul said, "Bring the burnt offering here to me, and the peace offerings." And he offered the burnt offering. 10 As soon as he had finished offering the burnt offering, behold, Samuel came. And Saul went out to meet him and greet him. 11 Samuel said, "What have you done?" And Saul said, "When I saw that the people were scattering from me, and that you did not come within the days appointed, and that the Philistines had mustered at Michmash, 12 I said, 'Now the Philistines will come down against me at Gilgal, and I have not sought the favor of the Lord.' So I forced myself, and offered the burnt offering." 13 And Samuel*

   Cardo- Palladius Street

   said to Saul, "You have done foolishly. You have not kept the command of the Lord your God, with which he commanded you. For then the Lord would have established your kingdom over Israel forever. 14 But now your kingdom shall not continue. The Lord has sought out a man after his own heart, and the Lord has commanded him to be prince over his people, because you have not kept what the Lord commanded you."

Northern Israel Sites

4. **Saul failed to obey God by not destroying God's enemies.**

   1 Samuel 15:1–3: And Samuel said to Saul, "The LORD sent me to anoint you king over his people Israel; now therefore listen to the words of the LORD. 2 Thus says the LORD of hosts, 'I have noted what Amalek did to Israel in opposing them on the way when they came up out of Egypt. 3 Now go and strike Amalek and devote to destruction all that they have. Do not spare them, but kill both man and woman, child and infant, ox and sheep, camel and donkey."

5. **Samuel confronts Saul's disobedience.**

   1 Samuel 15:22–23: And Samuel said, "Has the LORD as great delight in burnt offerings and sacrifices, as in obeying the voice of the LORD? Behold, to obey is better than sacrifice, and to listen than the fat of rams. 23 For rebellion is as the sin of divination, and presumption is as iniquity and idolatry. Because you have rejected the word of the LORD, he has also rejected you from being king."

   Amphitheater/Hippodrome

   Interestingly, it would be an Amalekite, whom Saul did not destroy, that would later kill him.

6. **In a heated battle with the Philistines, Saul disobeyed God and visited a witch of Endor.**

   1 Samuel 28:15–19: Then Samuel said to Saul, "Why have you disturbed me by bringing me up?" Saul answered, "I am in great distress, for the Philistines are warring against me, and God has turned away from me and answers me no more, either by prophets or by dreams. Therefore, I have summoned you to tell me what I shall do." 16 And Samuel said, "Why then do you ask me, since the Lord has turned from you and become your enemy? 17 The Lord has done to you as he spoke by me, for the Lord has torn the kingdom out of your hand and given it to your neighbor, David. 18 Because you did not obey the voice of the Lord and did not carry out his fierce wrath against Amalek, therefore the Lord has done this thing to you this day. 19 *Moreover, the Lord will give Israel also with you into the hand of the Philistines, and tomorrow you and your sons shall be with me. The Lord will give the army of Israel also into the hand of the Philistines."*

7. As a result of Saul's repeated disobedience, God took his life.

1 Samuel 31:1–13: *Now the Philistines fought against Israel, and the men of Israel fled before the Philistines and fell slain on Mount Gilboa. 2 And the Philistines overtook Saul and his sons, and the Philistines struck down Jonathan and Abinadab and Malchi-shua, the sons of Saul. 3 The battle pressed hard against Saul, and the archers found him, and he was badly wounded by the archers. 4 Then Saul said to his armor-bearer, "Draw*

Western Bathhouse & Sigma

your sword, and thrust me through with it, lest these uncircumcised come and thrust me through, and mistreat me." But his armor-bearer would not, for he feared greatly. Therefore, Saul took his own sword and fell upon it. 5 And when his armor-bearer saw that Saul was dead, he also fell upon his sword and died with him. 6 Thus Saul died, and his three sons, and his armor-bearer, and all his men, on the same day together. 7 And when the men of Israel who were on the other side of the valley and those beyond the Jordan saw that the men of Israel had fled and that Saul and his sons were dead, they abandoned their cities and fled. And the Philistines came and lived in them. 8 The next day, when the Philistines came to strip the slain, they found Saul and his three sons fallen on Mount Gilboa. 9 So they cut off his head and stripped off his armor and sent messengers throughout the land of the Philistines, to carry the good news to the house of their idols and to the people. 10 They put his armor in the temple of Ashtaroth, and they fastened his body to the **wall of Beth-shan**. *11 But when the inhabitants of Jabesh-gilead heard what the Philistines had done to Saul, 12 all the valiant men arose and went all night and took the body of Saul and the bodies of his sons from*

Northern Israel Sites

*the **wall of Beth-shan**, and they came to Jabesh and burned them there. 13 And they took their bones and buried them under the tamarisk tree in Jabesh and fasted seven days.*

Faith Lesson from Beth-Shean

1. Saul cared more about what people thought than what God thought of him.
2. He made big decisions without consulting the Lord.
3. Saul always had an excuse for his sin and disobedience.
4. We need to realize that obedience delights God more than asking forgiveness.
5. Rebellion and arrogance are the same as witchcraft because both attitudes fail to obey God and instead, seeks their own will and pleasure.

Beth-Shean ruins

6. Saul presumed upon God's grace. In other words, he believed he could disobey God, that God would just forgive him, and there would be no consequences. This attitude proved to be dangerous, sinful, and cost him his life and ministry.
7. Are we committed to submitting to God, or do we set ourselves up as our own authority like Saul?

Journal/Notes:

Beth-Shean Amphitheater/Hippodrome

Location

1. Beth-Shean, also known as Beit Shean or Bet She'an, was a major biblical and secular city for thousands of years.
2. It's located in the center of several main crossroads between the Jordan Valley and the Jezreel (Yizreel) Valley.
3. It's about 15 miles (25 km.) south of the southern tip of the Sea of Galilee and about 35 miles (55 km.) east of the Mediterranean Sea.

4. The Romans used the amphitheater/hippodrome in Bet-Shean for pleasure events, games with animals, and gladiator-type activities.
5. This arena seems to have served as both an amphitheater and hippodrome as it has openings into the arena from under the grandstands. It was common in Greek and Roman times that a city would have one stadium that could be used for both purposes because of financial and real estate reasons.
6. An amphitheater is different from a theater. An amphitheater has a full circle of seating, wherein a theater just has a semi-circle of seating.
7. The amphitheater/hippodrome was also used to persecute Christians during the early church period and later.
8. This amphitheater/hippodrome has underground rooms where wild beasts were released to devour people and other animals.
9. On many occasions, they were released in a game-like event where believers who refused to deny Christ were torn to pieces and eaten alive while the crowd roared in a frenzy.
10. It's sobering and gives a person chills to just think about it!

Northern Israel Sites

Historical Background

1. Beth-Shean was a key city long before the arrival of the Israelites because of its location. In the late Canaanite period (1600–1400 BC), the Egyptians ruled the area and the entire land of Israel.

2. Later, around 1000 BC, the Philistines also ruled the city for a time as they hung the body of King Saul on its walls after defeating the armies of Israel in the Battle of Gilboa.

Amphitheater/Hippodrome

3. When King David reigned (1010–970 BC), he conquered Beth-Shean, and it became part of Israel's territories.

4. Later, in around 732 BC, the Assyrian king, Tiglath-Pileser III, destroyed Beth-Shean and the northern Kingdom of Israel.

5. In the 4th century BC, Hellenistic (Greek) settlers established a city-state (polis) in Beth-Shean. During the Hellenistic period, the city was named Nisa Scythopolis.

6. In 63 BC, the city was conquered by the Romans and became one of the cities of the Decapolis – a group of cities with a Hellenistic-Roman cultural character, most of them in Transjordan. Beth-Shean was one of the key cities of the Roman Empire in this area south of Galilee.

Places of Interest

1. The Arena – Is derived from the word "sand." It's where the activities were carried out and was in the center.
2. Grandstands where the people were seated. The stadium's many seats have crumbled over the years, but it's estimated the seating capacity would have been between 10,000–20,000 people.
3. Entrance openings into the arena from under the grandstands.
4. Rooms under the grandstands where the animals and people

would wait before being released into the arena.

The Amphitheater/Hippodrome in the Bible

1. **Persecution was a common practice, and the Bible refers to what many believers faced.**

   Hebrews 11:35–38: *Some were tortured, refusing to accept release so that they might rise again to a better life. 36 Others suffered mocking and flogging, and even chains and imprisonment. 37 They were stoned, they were sawn in two, they were killed with the sword. They went about in skins of sheep and goats, destitute, afflicted, mistreated 38 of whom the world was not worthy, wandering about in deserts and mountains, and in dens and caves of the earth.*

   Acts 7 records how Stephen was one of the first to suffer early Christian persecution. He was stoned to death outside the gates for the faithful manner in which he preached the gospel. After this, a great persecution arose against all who professed belief in Christ as the Messiah.

   Acts 8:1: *And Saul approved of his [Stephen] execution. And there arose on that day a great persecution against the church in Jerusalem, and they were all scattered throughout the regions of Judea and Samaria, except the apostles.*

2. **History and tradition provide rich data regarding the believed fate of many of the apostles, along with other believers who suffered persecution for their faith in Christ**

Northern Israel Sites

during the early church period.

1. James the Great, the elder brother of John the Apostle, was beheaded in 44 AD.
2. Philip, who served in Upper Asia, was scourged in Phrygia, thrown into prison, and later crucified in 54 AD.

Looking out from an underground room

3. Matthew, the tax collector, served the Lord in Parthia and Ethiopia, where he was slain with a halberd (a shafted weapon with an ax-like cutting blade and a speared end) in the city of Nadabah in 60 AD.
4. James the Less, the brother of the Lord, served the church in Jerusalem and wrote the book of James. He suffered martyrdom at the age of 94 by being beaten and stoned by the Jews.
5. Matthias, the man who was chosen to replace Judas as an apostle, was stoned at Jerusalem and then beheaded.
6. Andrew, the brother of Peter, preached the gospel to many Asiatic nations and was crucified on a cross at Edessa. The ends of his cross were fixed transversely in the ground, thus the derivation of the term, Andrew's Cross.
7. Mark was converted to Christianity by Peter and served as his personal scribe. He was dragged to pieces and died by the people of Alexandria.
8. The Apostle Peter was sought by Nero to be put to death. Jerome wrote that Peter was crucified with his head down and his feet up because he thought himself unworthy to be crucified in the same way as Christ.
9. The Apostle Paul was persecuted all throughout his ministry. He was scourged, stoned, and finally, Nero had him beheaded by a sword.

10. Jude, the brother of James, commonly called Thaddeus, was crucified at Edessa in 72 AD.
11. Bartholomew preached in several countries and translated the Gospel of Matthew into the language of India. He was cruelly beaten and then crucified by impatient idolaters.

12. Thomas (doubting Thomas) preached the gospel in Parthia and India. His ministry caused the rage of the pagan priests, and he was martyred by being thrust through with a spear.
13. Luke, the author of Luke and Acts, traveled with Paul through various countries and was supposed to have been hanged on an olive tree by the idolatrous priests of Greece.
14. Simon the Zealot preached the gospel in Mauritania, Africa, and even Britain, where he was crucified in 74 AD.
15. John, the apostle whom Jesus loved, was sent from Ephesus to Rome, where he was put into a cauldron of boiling oil. He escaped by a miracle without injury but was then banished to the Isle of Patmos, where he wrote the book of Revelation. Nerva, Domitian's successor, said he was the only apostle who escaped a violent death.

3. **There are ten persecutions mentioned in *Foxe's Book of Martyrs* that are quite gruesome.**
   1. The first mass persecution occurred under Nero in 64 AD. He was the sixth emperor of Rome and is remembered as the one who set Rome aflame and then blamed the Christians for the deaths and destruction caused by the fire. He had some Christians sewn up in skins of wild beasts and thrown to the dogs. Some Christians were dressed in shirts made stiff with wax, fixed to axletrees, and set on fire alongside streets and in Nero's gardens in order to illuminate them. Rather than diminishing the spirit of Christianity, this persecution increased the devotion and commitment of Christians instead.

Northern Israel Sites

2. The second persecution happened under Domitian in 81 AD. Anything bad that happened like famine, pestilence, or earthquakes he blamed on the Christians and put them to death.

3. The third persecution occurred under Trajan in 108 AD. Christians were beaten, beheaded, and devoured by wild beasts, causing about ten thousand Christians to be put to death.

Inside an underground room

4. The fourth persecution took place under Marcus Aurelius Antoninus in 162 AD.

5. The fifth persecution is credited to Severus in 192 AD. Christians were burned at the stake, had hot tar poured on their heads, beheaded, placed in boiling water, and ravaged by wild beasts.

6. The sixth persecution took place under Maximus in 235 AD. At this time, numerous Christians were slain without trial and buried indiscriminately in mass graves, sometimes 50 or 60 cast into a pit together.

7. The seventh persecution happened under Decius in 249 AD. The main person martyred was Fabian, the bishop of Rome, who was beheaded on January 20, 250 AD.

8. The eighth persecution occurred under Valerian in 257 AD. Once again, every manner of torture was used to mock those claiming to be Christians. Persecution was also used for the entertainment of the rulers and their guests.

9. The ninth persecution occurred under Aurelian in 274 AD, when Felix, bishop of Rome, was martyred.

10. The tenth persecution took place under Diocletian in 303 AD. This was commonly called the Era of the Martyrs. Persecutions were carried out with racks, scourges, swords, daggers, crosses, poisons, and famine.

11. Today, there are more martyrs for Christ than there have ever been at any time in the history of the church. Many of these take place in the Middle East and go unnoticed by the public eye.

Underground rooms

According to BBC News, there are around 100,000–250,000 Christians who are martyred every year.

Faith Lesson from Beth-Shean Amphitheater/Hippodrome

1. God used persecution to give more validity, power, and meaning to the message of the gospel.
2. We show the world the value of our faith by what it cost us to keep and obey it.
3. During the years between 313 and 325 AD, Constantine, the Roman Emperor of that time, became a Christian and later declared Christianity the religion of the Roman Empire.
4. It was the persecution of Christians that God used most to convert the Roman Empire to Christianity.
5. Through persecution, God changed the religion of the most powerful nation on the earth to Christianity.
6. The church has seen its greatest growth and maturity during the periods it was persecuted the most.
7. We are nearing a time when it is going to cost us to follow Christ as well.

Hebrews 12:1–4: *Therefore, since we are* **surrounded by so great a cloud of witnesses**, *let us also lay aside every weight, and sin which clings so closely, and let us run with endurance the race that is set before us, 2 looking to Jesus, the founder and perfecter of our faith, who for the joy that was set before him endured the cross,* *despising the shame, and is seated at the right hand of the throne of God. 3 Consider him who endured from sinners such hostility against himself, so that you may not grow weary or fainthearted. 4 In your struggle against sin, you have not yet resisted to the point of shedding your blood.*

8. Are we willing to suffer for our faith?
9. What does it cost us to follow Christ?

10. Do we stand firm on God's Word despite opposition?
11. Do we allow ourselves to be persuaded to compromise our faith because of pressure from our peers?
12. Do we subtly deny Christ in moments when we're around people who don't share our faith?
13. The only thing these Christians who died in this amphitheater here in Beth-Shean would have had to do to save their lives and not be shredded to pieces by the wild beast was to deny Christ.
14. But they didn't, and today they have a special reward in heaven for being a martyr.
15. How about us? Are we willing to do the same?

Journal/Notes:

Caesarea Philippi

Location

1. Few other places in Scripture provide so much meaning by understanding the location.
2. It was here that Peter made the divinely inspired declaration the Jesus was the Christ, the Son of the living God.
3. Caesarea Philippi was an impressive Greco-Roman city near a huge spring that comes out of a cave and is one of the main sources of the Jordan River.
4. It's about 30 miles (48 km.) north of the Sea of Galilee and is at the foothills of Mount Hermon.
5. It was close to a "high place" where Jeroboam set up a golden calf for the northern tribes of Israel to worship, which led to their downfall.
6. In around 1000 AD, an earthquake collapsed part of the cave and changed the water flow. Now the water comes out of the ground below the cave.

Historical Background

1. This place has been associated with intense false god worship and evil for many years.
2. Baal worship took place here during the period of the kings of Israel.
3. King Jeroboam set up a golden calf not far from here and commanded all the Israelites in this area to worship it.
4. Later, under the Greeks, it became the key place of worship to the fertility god, Pan. Pan was a half-human, half-goat-like creature.
5. Then the Romans incorporated it into a place of false god worship

as well.

6. Caesarea Philippi was originally called Panion or Panias, after the Greek god Pan. Later it became known as Banias.
7. Herod the Great's son, Philip, established it as the capital of his territory and named it Caesarea to honor the emperor of Rome. It became a large flourishing Roman city.
8. It was known as Caesarea Philippi to distinguish it from other cities with the same name.
9. During the time of Christ, there were 5 main areas of worship to false gods that took place here.
    - Herod the Great built a temple right at the mouth of this enormous spring to honor Augustus Caesar.
    - A courtyard area to the worship of Pan.
    - A temple dedicated to the false god Zeus.
    - An upper Tomb Temple of the Dancing Goats.
    - A lower Tomb Temple of the Dancing Goats.
10. It was a worldwide gathering place of worship to numerous false gods.
11. It was literally considered the "Gate of the Underworld (Hades)" by the known world at that time.

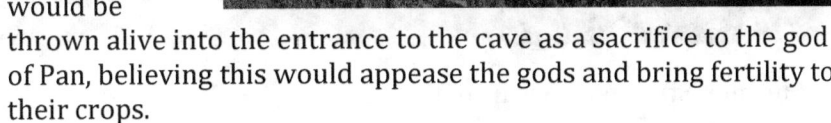

12. Children would be thrown alive into the entrance to the cave as a sacrifice to the god of Pan, believing this would appease the gods and bring fertility to their crops.
13. Some even believe that men would mate with goats in the courtyard of Pan and on the Tomb Temples in ritualistic fertility acts believing this would help their crops. They would also have goats mating with goats as well in these areas.
14. It was a sick cesspool of evil and represented the worst Satan and sinful humanity could offer.
15. The disciples were very uncomfortable coming to this eerie,

demonic, dark place, and no good Jew would have even considered coming here.

16. However, Jesus purposefully brought His disciples here to embed within their hearts the imperative truth of who He was, what the mission of His church would be, and the astounding power His church would have over evil through Him.

Places of Interest

1. Cave Entrance (place the large spring was located)
2. Temple of Augustus
3. Courtyard of Pan
4. Temple of Zeus
5. Upper Tomb Temple of the Dancing Goats
6. Lower Tomb Temple of the Dancing Goats

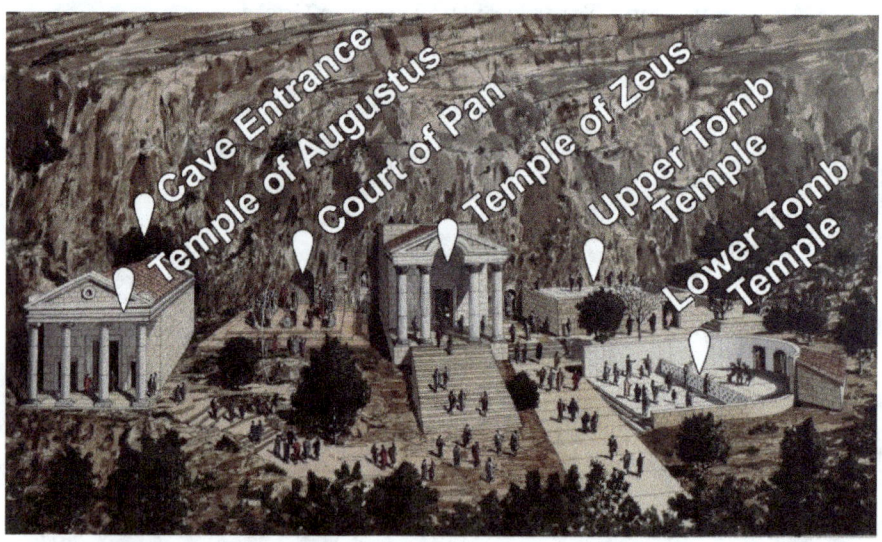

7. Hermon Stream (flows from the cave entrance)
8. Byzantine Church
9. Cardo
10. Moat
11. Church
12. Crusader Church
13. Palace of Agrippa II

14. Flour Mill
15. Roman Bridge

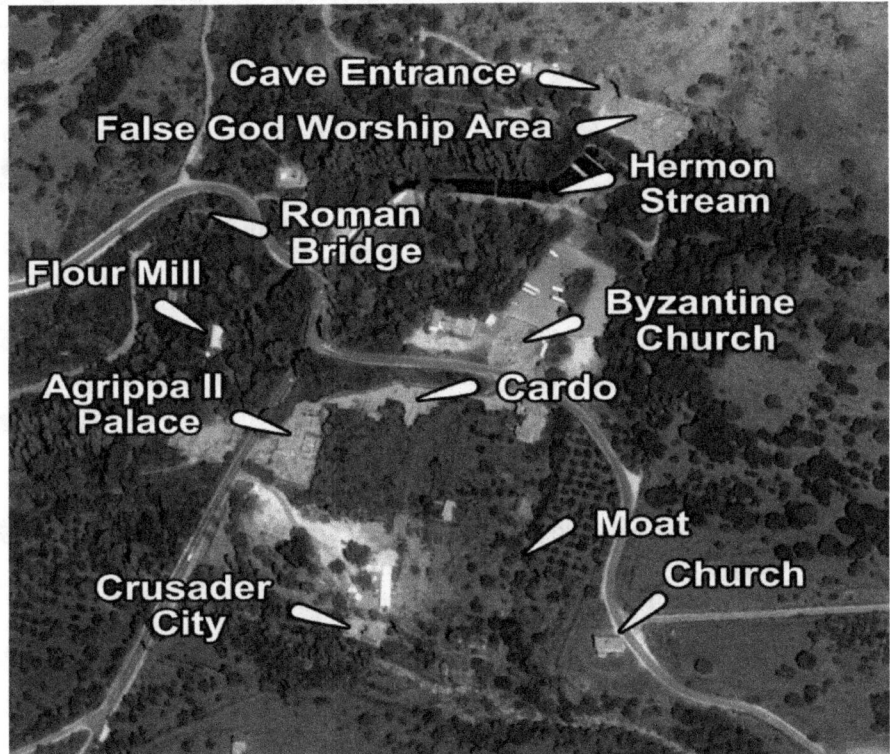

Caesarea Philippi in the Bible

1. **Peter's confession about the identity of Christ.**

   Matthew 16:13–16: *Now when Jesus came into the district of **Caesarea Philippi**, he asked his disciples, **"Who do people say that the Son of Man is?"** 14 And they said, "Some say John the Baptist, others say Elijah, and others Jeremiah or one of the prophets." 15 He said to them, "But who do you say that I am?" 16 Simon Peter replied, **"You are the Christ, the Son of the living God."***

   - To properly understand the meaning of this passage, we must understand the big question Christ asked and the purpose for which He asked it.
   - The question was about who Christ was, His identity, and His essence.
   - In contrast to all the false gods being worshiped at this site,

Christ established that He was the only true and living God that should be worshiped.

2. Peter's confession was a direct revelation from God.

Matthew 16:17: *And Jesus answered him, "Blessed are you, Simon Bar-Jonah! For flesh and blood has not revealed this to you, but my Father who is in heaven."*

3. Christ will build His Church.

Matthew 16:18: *And I tell you, you are Peter [petros – small pebble], and on this rock [petra – large, massive rock],* **I will build my church***, and the gates of hell shall not prevail against it.*

This passage has had two main interpretations throughout history. The Roman Catholic Church claims that the rock upon which Christ will build His Church is Peter, upon which they build the papacy. Evangelicals claim that the rock is Christ, based upon Peter's confession.

Evidence that the rock is Christ, not Peter:

- Christ used the word ***petros*** in describing Peter. He used the word ***petra*** in describing upon whom He would build His Church. Christ certainly wouldn't build His Church upon a pebble.

- Christ didn't say He would build His Church upon Peter because He says, "*Upon this rock.*" He didn't say to Peter, "*Upon you.*"

- Peter had three significant failures in his ministry life: (1) In Matthew 16:23, just shortly after Peter's confession of who Christ

Courtyard to false gods

was, Christ rebuked Peter and told him, "*Get behind me Satan.*" (2) Peter denied Christ shortly before Christ's crucifixion. (3) Paul rebuked Peter in Galatians 2:11 in front of everyone for a serious matter regarding the gospel. Christ certainly wouldn't build His Church upon a frail human.

- Christ is referred to as the Cornerstone and foundation of the Church.
- Peter understood he was not the rock upon which Christ would build His church as he states in 1 Peter 2:4–6:

    As you come to him, a living stone *rejected by men but in the sight of God chosen and precious, 5 you yourselves like living stones are being built up as a spiritual house, to be a holy priesthood, to offer spiritual sacrifices acceptable to God through Jesus Christ. 6 For it stands in Scripture:* "**Behold, I am laying in Zion a stone, a cornerstone** *chosen and precious, and whoever believes in him will not be put to shame.*"

    The rock upon which the Church is being built is Christ, the Cornerstone.

4. **The Gates of Hell will not prevail against Christ's Church.**

    Matthew 16:18: *And I tell you, you are Peter, and on this rock, I will build my church, and the **gates of hell shall not prevail against it***.

    - Christ purposefully took His disciples to this evil Pagan place to show them that His Church would be so powerful that the gates of hell wouldn't be able to prevail or stand against it.
    - Gates were used in the ancient world for defensive purposes. They were used to keep an enemy from entering a certain place.

    Court of Pan

    - This means that the church is on the offense, and the gates of hell will not be able to withstand its entry and power.
    - Contrary to what some might believe, the church is not on defense in a stationary mode standing its ground.
    - God has designed His Church to be in the world, but not of it. This means we should be involved in influencing the world for Christ, not retreating and hiding from it.

- Christ wants His Church involved in society and reaching every hidden corner of it for Him.

5. **From Caesarea Philippi, Jesus began His journey to Jerusalem to be crucified**.

   Matthew 16:21–23: *From that time Jesus began to show his disciples that he must go to Jerusalem and suffer many things from the elders and chief priests and scribes, and be killed, and on the third day be raised. 22 And Peter took him aside and began to rebuke him, saying, "Far be it from you, Lord! This shall never happen to you." 23 But he turned and said to Peter,* **"Get behind me, Satan!** *You are a hindrance to me. For you are not setting your mind on the things of God, but on the things of man."*

6. **Christ teaches about the commitment level He demands from the disciples of His Church.**

   Matthew 16:24–27: *Then Jesus told his disciples, "If anyone would come after me, let him deny himself and take up his cross and follow me. 25 For whoever would save his life will lose it, but whoever loses his life for my sake will find it. 26 For what will it profit a man if he gains the whole world and forfeits his soul? Or what*

   Hermon Stream that flows from the cave

   shall a man give in return for his soul? 27 For the Son of Man is going to come with his angels in the glory of his Father, and then he will repay each person according to what he has done."

Faith Lesson from Caesarea Philippi

1. Are we on the offense and influencing our world for Christ, or are we retreating and hiding out?
2. Do we truly believe that Christ and His Church are more powerful than Satan and the culture we live in?
3. Do we know God's Word so we can use it effectively in advancing

the truth against the lies of Satan and the world?
4. Do we understand the spiritual battles that are taking place today?
   - The belief that truth is just what each person believes it to be and what works for them personally.
   - The belief that feelings and emotions determine truth and what's right and wrong.
   - The belief that if it feels good, it must be right, or if it makes me happy, it can't be wrong.
   - The belief that there are no absolute standards of right and wrong that apply to everyone.
   - The belief that truth is rigid, intolerant, and judgmental.
   - The belief that if we speak the truth of God's Word to someone, we are judging them and intolerant.

Byzantine Church

5. Are we willing to pay the cost Christ demands to be His disciples?

Journal/Notes:

Caesarea Maritime

Location

Caesarea is located on the beautiful Mediterranean Sea about 35 miles (56 km.) north of Joppa.

Historical Background

1. Caesarea was built by Herod the Great from about 25 to 13 BC as the port city called "Caesarea Maritime."
2. It was named after the Roman Emperor, Augustus Caesar.
3. King Herod the Great was the one who had all the children 2 years and younger slaughtered in Bethlehem in his attempt to kill Christ. He was a jealous king who feared losing his power and control.
4. King Herod built Caesarea out of nothing and was a master builder. Some of his major building projects included:
   - This seaport of Caesarea
   - An enlarged Temple Mount platform and temple in Jerusalem.
   - Masada
   - The Herodian by Bethlehem.
   - Cave of the Patriarchs in Hebron.
5. He was known for his building ventures, and no one equaled him in this respect.
6. Caesarea was the largest seaport in the Roman Empire during the time of Herod.
7. Caesarea was the capital of Israel during the time of Christ and during the whole Roman occupation of Israel.

Places of Interest

1. Crusader Fortress Entrance

Northern Israel Sites

2. Crusader Fortress
3. Caesarea Harbor
4. Caesarea Historic Port
5. Governor's Palace
6. Roman Toilet
7. Mosaic Hall
8. Hippodrome
9. Promontory Palace
10. Caesarea Columns
11. Roman Theater
12. Submerged Garden Castle
13. Pontius Pilate Stone
14. Paul Appeals to Caesar Marker

Caesarea in the Bible

1. **After the Apostle Paul received Christ, he was sent to Tarsus from this seaport.**

   Acts 9:30: *And when the brothers learned this, they brought him down to **Caesarea** and sent him off to Tarsus.*

2. **Cornelius, the first Gentile to receive the Holy Spirit, lived here.**

   Acts 10:1–8: *At **Caesarea** there was a man named Cornelius, a centurion of what was known as the Italian Cohort, 2 a devout man who feared God with all his household, gave alms generously to the people, and prayed continually to God. 3 About the*  *ninth hour of the day he saw clearly in a vision an angel of God come in and say to him, "Cornelius." 4 And he stared at him in terror and said, "What is it, Lord?" And he said to him, "Your prayers and your alms have ascended as a memorial before God. 5 And now send men to Joppa and bring one Simon who is called Peter. 6 He is lodging with one Simon, a tanner, whose house is by the sea." 7 When the angel who spoke to him had departed, he called two of his servants and a devout soldier from among those who attended him, 8 and having related everything to them, he sent them to Joppa.*

3. **Caesarea was the place where the Holy Spirit was given to the Gentiles.**

   Acts 10:44–48: *While Peter was still saying these things, the Holy Spirit fell on all who heard the word. 45 And the believers from among the circumcised who had come with Peter were amazed, because the gift of the Holy Spirit was poured out even on the Gentiles. 46 For they were hearing them speaking in tongues and extolling God. Then Peter declared, 47 "Can anyone withhold water for baptizing these people, who have received the Holy Spirit just as we have?" 48 And he commanded them to be baptized in the name of*

Jesus Christ. Then they asked him to remain for some days.

4. **King Herod Agrippa the 1st, the son of Herod the Great, met his death in Caesarea.**

   Acts 12:21–24: *On an appointed day Herod put on his royal robes, took his seat upon the throne, and delivered an oration to them. 22 And the people were shouting, "The voice of a god, and not of a man!" 23 Immediately an angel of the Lord struck him down, because he did not give God the glory, and he was eaten by worms and breathed his last. 24 But the word of God increased and multiplied.*

5. **Philip the Evangelist lived in Caesarea.**

   Acts 21:8: *On the next day we departed and came to **Caesarea**, and we entered the house of Philip the evangelist, who was one of the seven, and stayed with him.*

6. **The Apostle Paul sailed to and from Caesarea on his missionary travels.**

   Acts 21:7–8: *When we had finished the voyage from Tyre, we arrived at Ptolemais, and we greeted the brothers and stayed with them for one day. 8 On the next day we departed and came*

   *to **Caesarea**, and we entered the house of Philip the evangelist, who was one of the seven, and stayed with him.*

7. **The Apostle Paul stood trial here for his faith.**

   Acts 23:33–35: *When they had come to **Caesarea** and delivered the letter to the governor, they presented Paul also before him. 34 On reading the letter, he asked what province he was from. And when he learned that he was from Cilicia, 35 he said, "I will give you a hearing when your accusers arrive." And he commanded him to be guarded in Herod's Praetorium.*

8. **The Apostle Paul was imprisoned here 2 years because of his faith.**

   Acts 24:27: *When two years had elapsed, Felix was succeeded by Porcius Festus. And desiring to do the Jews a favor, Felix left Paul in prison.*

   It's possible that Paul wrote some of the Prison Epistles in Caesarea during the 2 years he spent here in prison.

9. **After spending 2 years of imprisonment in Caesarea, the Apostle Paul sailed from Caesarea to Rome, where he stood trial for his faith.**

   Acts 25:8, 11: *Paul argued in his defense, "Neither against the law of the Jews, nor against the temple, nor against Caesar have I committed any offense."* Paul then declares in verse 11: *"I appeal to Caesar."*

Faith Lesson from Caesarea

1. The Holy Spirit was given to the Gentiles here. This shows that God loves all people from all races and backgrounds and wants them to be saved.

2. Paul spent 2 years in prison here because of his faithfulness to Christ. It's possible he wrote some of the Prison Letters while here. We, too, should be willing to suffer like Paul for the advancement of the gospel.

3. God opposes the proud and caused King Herod Agrippa the 1st, the son of Herod the Great, to meet his death here because of his arrogance. We should be certain we always give God the glory for what He does through us and avoid pride in our lives.

Journal/Notes:

Northern Israel Sites

Cana

Location

Cana is in the northern part of Israel in the Galilee area. It's about 11 miles (17 km.) southwest of the Sea of Galilee, about 4 miles (6.4 km.) northeast of Nazareth, and about 22 miles (35 km.) inland from the Mediterranean Sea.

Historical Background

1. Cana's actual location is uncertain, with at least three possible candidates.
2. However, at the Wedding Church, the Franciscans have relied on the testimony of early pilgrims, including Jerome, as being the authentic site. Therefore, they established themselves here in 1641.
3. The Franciscans also believe excavations beneath their present church, dating from the early 1900s, confirm the existence of an early place of worship. They believe it's possible it was a Jewish-Christian synagogue.
4. Beneath the present Franciscan Wedding Church were found remains of dwellings dating back to the 1st century. An ancient basilica with three arch vaults in a cross-like form was also discovered. Additionally, in a crypt, a small stone cistern was found fitted into a flagstone floor.
5. Not far from the Wedding Church is the Greek Orthodox Church of the Marriage Feast. It possesses two large stone jars believed to be two of the original water pots used when Christ turned the water into wine.
6. The town also has a chapel dedicated to Bartholomew, whom some scholars identify with Nathanael of Cana.

Places of Interest

1. Franciscan Wedding Church

2. Greek Orthodox Church
3. Nathanael Bartholomew Church
4. Cana Baptist Church

Cana in the Bible

1. Jesus changed water into wine.

John 2:1–11: *On the third day there was a wedding at Cana in Galilee, and the mother of Jesus was there. 2 Jesus also was invited to the wedding with his disciples. 3 When the wine ran out, the mother of Jesus said to him, "They have no wine." 4 And Jesus said to her, "Woman, what does this have to do with me? My hour has not yet come." 5 His mother said to the servants, "Do whatever he tells you." 6 Now there were six stone water jars there for the Jewish rites of purification, each holding twenty or thirty gallons. 7 Jesus said to the servants, "Fill the jars with water." And they filled them up to the brim. 8 And he said to them, "Now draw some out and take it to the master of the feast." So they took it. 9 When the master of the feast tasted the water now become wine, and did not know where it came from (though the servants who had drawn the water knew), the master of the feast called the bridegroom 10 and said to him, "Everyone serves the good wine first, and when people have drunk freely, then the poor wine. But you have kept the good wine until now." 11* **This, the first of his signs, Jesus did at Cana in Galilee**, *and manifested his glory. And his disciples believed in him.*

2. **Jesus also healed an official's son in Cana.**

   John 4:46–54: *So he came again to Cana in Galilee, where he had made the water wine. And at Capernaum, there was an official whose son was ill. 47 When this man heard that Jesus had come from Judea to Galilee, he went to him and asked him to come down and heal his son, for he was at the point of death. 48 So Jesus said to him, "Unless you see signs and wonders you will not believe." 49 The official said to him, "Sir, come down before my child dies." 50 Jesus said to him, "Go; your son will live." The man believed the word that Jesus spoke to him and went on his way. 51 As he was going down, his servants met him and told him that his son was recovering. 52 So he asked them the hour when he began to get better, and they said to him, "Yesterday at the seventh hour the fever left him." 53 The father knew that was the hour when Jesus had said to him, "Your son will live." And he himself believed, and all his household. 54 This was now the second sign that Jesus did when he had come from Judea to Galilee.*

   Wedding Church

3. **Nathanael, one of the close followers of Christ and close friend (or possibly a brother) of the Apostle Philip, was from Cana.**

   John 21:2: *Simon Peter, Thomas,* **Nathanael from Cana** *in Galilee, the sons of Zebedee, and two other disciples were together.*

4. **The Apostle Philip led Nathanael, who was from Cana, to Christ.**

   John 1:43–51: *The next day Jesus decided to go to Galilee. He found Philip and said to him, "Follow me." 44 Now Philip was from Bethsaida, the city of Andrew and Peter. 45 Philip found Nathanael and said to him, "We have found him of whom Moses in the Law and also the prophets wrote, Jesus of Nazareth, the son of Joseph." 46 Nathanael said to him, "Can anything good come out of Nazareth?"*

Philip said to him, "Come and see." 47 Jesus saw Nathanael coming toward him and said of him, "Behold, an Israelite indeed, in whom there is no deceit!" 48 Nathanael said to him, "How do you know me?" Jesus answered him, "Before Philip called you, when you were under the fig tree, I saw you." 49 Nathanael answered him, "Rabbi, you are the Son of God! You are the King of Israel!" 50 Jesus answered him, "Because I said to you, 'I saw you under the fig tree,' do you believe? You will see greater things than these." 51 And he said to him, "Truly, truly, I say to you, you will see heaven opened, and the angels of God ascending and descending on the Son of Man."

Greek Orthodox Church

Faith Lesson from Cana

1. Christ performed His first public miracle in Cana to authenticate and show that He was the promised Messiah. Do we believe Christ was God in the flesh and the true Messiah?
2. Christ honored the request of His mother in turning the water into wine. Do we honor our parents as Christ did, and as God commands?
3. Jesus also healed an official's son here in Cana. Do we believe Christ can still do miracles today in our own lives?
4. If you could ask Christ for one miracle, what would it be?
5. In the same way Philip led Nathanael to Christ, do we lead others to Christ?
6. Christ turned water into wine to fulfill many Old Testament prophecies that proved He was the Messiah. Do we believe Christ is the Messiah, and have we placed our trust in Him as our Savior?

Journal/Notes:

Dan

Location

1. The city of Dan was in the northernmost part of Israel, about 24 miles (38 km.) north of the Sea of Galilee.
2. It's a well-watered lush area superb for agriculture.

Historical Background

1. The tribe of Dan failed to take the original territory allotted to them, so they captured and moved to this area (Judg. 18).
2. When referring to all Israel, the phrase "From Dan to Beersheba" was commonly used.

   1 Kings 4:25: *Judah and Israel lived safely, every man under his vine and under his fig tree, **from Dan even to Beersheba**, all the days of Solomon.*

3. Just after Solomon's reign, the kingdom of Israel was divided because Solomon turned from the Lord and introduced the worship of false gods into the nation.

   1 Kings 11:1–2: *Now King Solomon loved many foreign women along with the daughter of Pharaoh: Moabite, Ammonite, Edomite, Sidonian, and Hittite women, 2 from the nations concerning which the Lord had said to the sons of Israel, "You shall not associate with them, nor shall they associate with you, for they will surely **turn your heart away** after their gods." Solomon held fast to these in love.*

   1 Kings 11:6–11: *Solomon did what was evil in the sight of the Lord, and did not follow the Lord fully, as David his father had done. 7 Then Solomon built a high place for Chemosh the detestable idol of Moab, on the mountain which is east of Jerusalem, and for Molech the detestable idol of the sons of Ammon. 8 Thus also he did for all*

*his foreign wives, who burned incense and sacrificed to their gods. 9 Now the Lord was angry with Solomon **because his heart was turned away from the Lord**, the God of Israel, who **had appeared to him twice**, 10 and had commanded him concerning this thing, that he should **not go after other gods**; but he did not observe what the Lord had commanded. 11 So the Lord said to Solomon, "Because you have done this, and you have not kept My covenant and My statutes, which I have commanded you, I will surely **tear the kingdom from you**, and will give it to your servant."*

4. Rehoboam was given the southern 2 tribes of Israel (called Judah from this time forward), and Jeroboam received the northern 10 tribes of Israel (called Israel from this time forward).

Places of Interest

1. Entrance
2. Dan River
3. Jeroboam's Golden Calf High Place
4. City Ruins
5. Israelite Gate
6. Canaanite Gate
7. Shallow Pool

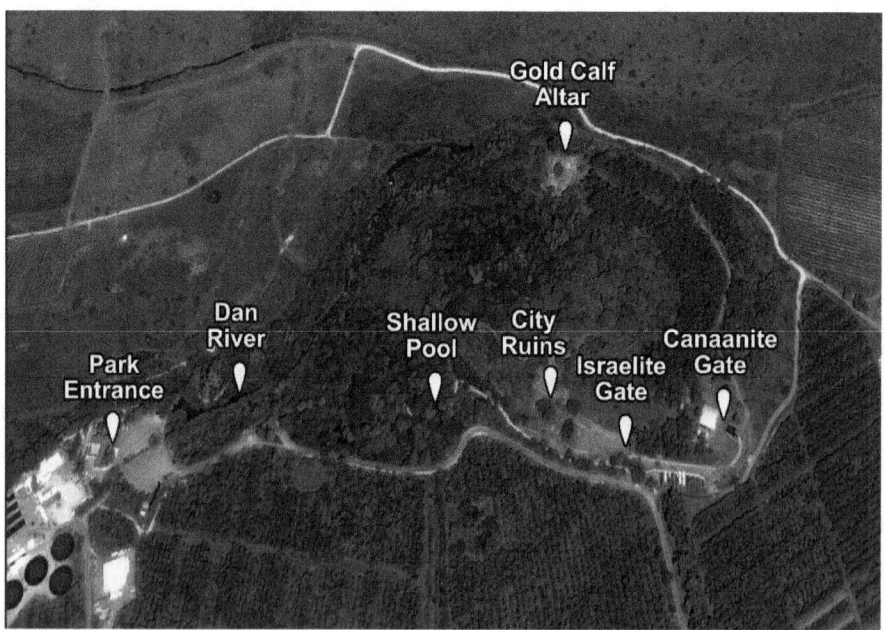

Northern Israel Sites

City of Dan in the Bible

1. **God appeared to Jeroboam and promised to bless him if he would serve Him.**

   1 Kings 11:38: *Then it will be, that if you listen to all that I command you and walk in My ways, and do what is right in My sight by observing My statutes and My commandments, as My servant David did, then I will be with you and build you an enduring house as I built for David, and I will give Israel to you.*

2. **Jeroboam turned away from the Lord and built golden calves in Bethel and Dan.**

   1 Kings 12:25–31: *Then Jeroboam built Shechem in the hill country of Ephraim, and lived there. And he went out from there and built Penuel. 26 Jeroboam said in his heart, "Now the kingdom will return to the house of David. 27 If this people go up to offer sacrifices in the house of the Lord at Jerusalem, then the heart of this people will return to their lord, even to Rehoboam king of Judah; and they will kill me and return to Rehoboam king of Judah." 28 So the king consulted, and made **two golden calves**, and he said to them, "It is too much for you to go up to Jerusalem; behold your gods, O Israel, that brought you up from the land of Egypt." 29 He set **one in Bethel**, and the other he put in **Dan**. 30 Now this thing became a sin, for the people went to worship before the one as far as **Dan**. 31 And he made **houses on high places**, and made priests from among all the people who were not of the sons of Levi.*

   Golden Calf Altar

3. **After a severe warning from God, Jeroboam continued in sin. The worship of false gods would eventually seal the doom of the northern 10 tribes of Israel.**

   1 Kings 13:33–34: *Even after this, Jeroboam did not change his evil ways, but once more appointed priests for the high places from all*

sorts of people. Anyone who wanted to become a priest he consecrated for the high places. 34 This was the sin of the house of Jeroboam that led to its **downfall and to its destruction** from the face of the earth.

4. **The sin of Jeroboam became a pattern that the rest of the kings of Israel would follow.**

   1 Kings 15:33–34: *In the third year of Asa king of Judah, Baasha son of Ahijah became king of all Israel in Tirzah, and he reigned twenty-four years. 34 He did evil in the eyes of the LORD,* **walking in the ways of Jeroboam** *and in his sin, which he had caused Israel to commit.*

   1 Kings 16:26: *He [Omri]* **walked in all the ways of Jeroboam** *son of Nebat and in his sin, which he had caused Israel to commit, so that they provoked the LORD, the God of Israel, to anger by their worthless idols.*

5. **In 722 BC, as judgment from God for their continual disobedience, the 10 northern tribes of Israel were deported by the Assyrian Empire.**

6. **Eighty years later, Josiah became King of Judah and chose to follow God with all his heart. As a result of finding and reading the Scriptures, he led one of the most significant revivals Israel ever experienced.**

   2 Kings 22:1–2: *Josiah was eight years old when he became king, and he reigned in Jerusalem thirty-one years. His mother's name was Jedidah daughter of Adaiah; she was from Bozkath. 2 He did what was right in the eyes of the LORD and walked in all the ways of his father David, not turning aside to the right or to the left.*

   Israelite City Gate

   2 Kings 23:25: *Before him,* **there was no king like him who turned to the Lord with all his heart and with all his soul and**

Northern Israel Sites

with all his might, *according to all the law of Moses; nor did any like him arise after him.*

7. **As a result of Josiah's obedience, he renewed the covenant of the Lord with Israel and destroyed the golden calves Jeroboam had erected.**

   2 Kings 23:15: *Furthermore, the altar that was at **Bethel** and the **high place** which Jeroboam the son of Nebat, who made Israel sin, had made, even that altar and the high place he broke down. Then he demolished its stones, ground them to dust, and burned the Asherah.*

   2 Kings 23:19: *Josiah also removed all the houses of the **high places** which were in the **cities of Samaria**, which the kings of Israel had made provoking the Lord; and he did to them just as he had done in Bethel.*

Faith Lesson from the city of Dan

1. Despite God supernaturally revealing Himself two times to Solomon, he turned away from the Lord in his latter years. There is a tendency to grow apathetic the longer we are Christians. Are you apathetic and lukewarm in your relationship with God?

2. Despite God supernaturally revealing himself two times to Jeroboam, he turned his back on God and built altars to false gods all throughout the land. God

   Dan River

   gives grace to each person to receive and obey Him, but those who reject Him and His grace will be judged accordingly.

3. The sin of Jeroboam became a pattern that the rest of the kings of the northern tribes of Israel followed. What kind of example are we? Are we following the sinful patterns of our parents and those around us?

4. In 722 BC, the 10 northern tribes of Israel were deported because of their refusal to return to God.

5. The worship of false gods at Bethel and Dan became the downfall of the northern tribes of Israel. False gods and idols can be anything we make more important in our lives than God. Do you have any idols in your life?

6. Josiah chose to follow God with all his heart and tore down the two golden calf altars Jeroboam had set up. Do we follow God with all our heart like Josiah, and work with God to tear down the lies and false philosophies of Satan and the world with God's Word (2 Cor. 10:4–5)?

City ruins

Journal/Notes:

Northern Israel Sites

Gideon's Spring

Location

Gideon's Spring, or also known as Harod Spring, is located in the fertile Jezreel Valley about 26 miles (42 km.) from the Mediterranean Sea and about 17 miles (28 km.) south of the Sea of Galilee. Just to the south of Gideon's Spring are the Gilboa Mountains.

Historical Background

1. The period of the Judges saw the nation of Israel experience many cycles of obedience and disobedience.
2. They would walk with God for a bit and then fall away.
3. One verse is repeated several times in the book of Judges that summarizes the mentality of their day: *"In those days there was no king in Israel; everyone did what was right in his own eyes"* (Judg. 17:6, 21:25).
4. In order to bring the nation of Israel back to Himself, God would send them oppressors to make their lives difficult.
5. As a result, the Israelites would look to the Lord, and He would send them a deliverer, or also known as a Judge.
6. Gideon was one of these deliverers that God raised up to deliver the Israelites out of the hand of the Midianites who were oppressing Israel at that time.
7. There were a total of 13 Judges or Deliverers in the book of Judges.
8. Gideon was the 6th Judge.

Places of Interest

1. Hill of Moreh: Hill area where the Midianites camped.
2. Midianite Camp
3. Jezreel Valley

4. Battle Area
5. Gideon's Spring – Area where Gideon chose 300 men for battle.
6. Gilboa Mountains – Where the Israelites hid out.
7. Hankin House Museum – Located above the spring entrance.

Gideon's Spring in the Bible

1. **God gave the Israelites into the hands of the Midianites because they abandoned and disobeyed Him.**

   Judges 6:1–6: *Then the sons of Israel did what was evil in the sight of the Lord; and the Lord gave them into the hands of Midian seven years. 2 The power of Midian prevailed against Israel. Because of Midian the sons of Israel made for themselves the dens which were in the mountains and the caves and the strongholds. 3 For it was when Israel had sown, that the Midianites would come up with the Amalekites and the sons of the east and go against them. 4 So they would camp against them and destroy the produce of the earth as far as Gaza, and leave no sustenance in Israel as well as no sheep, ox, or donkey. 5 For they would come up with their livestock and their* tents, they would come in like locusts for number, both they and their camels were innumerable; and they came into the land to devastate it. 6 So Israel was brought very low because of Midian, and the sons of Israel cried to the Lord.*

2. **God hears the prayers of the Israelites and decides to deliver them.**

   Judges 6:7–10: *Now it came about when the sons of Israel cried to the Lord on account of Midian, 8 that the Lord sent a prophet to the sons of Israel, and he said to them, "Thus says the Lord, the God of Israel, 'It was I who brought you up from Egypt and brought you out from the house of slavery. 9 I delivered you from the hands of the Egyptians and from the hands of all your oppressors, and dispossessed them before you and gave you their land, 10 and I said to you, I am the Lord your God; you shall not fear the gods of the Amorites in whose land you live. But you have not obeyed Me.'"*

3. **God visits Gideon through an angel and chooses to deliver the Israelites through him.**

   Judges 6:11–12: *Then the angel of the Lord came and sat under the oak that was in Ophrah, which belonged to Joash the Abiezrite as his son **Gideon** was beating out wheat in the winepress in order to save it from the Midianites. 12 The angel of the Lord appeared to him and said to him, "The Lord is with you, O valiant warrior."*

4. **Gideon responds by saying that his family was the least in the tribe of Manasseh and that he was the youngest in his family (Judg. 6:15). This is similar to the response of Moses when God called him.**

5. **God allows the angel to show Gideon a couple of miracles to prove God will help him.**

   Judges 6:21: *Then the angel of the Lord put out the end of the staff that was in his hand and touched the meat and the unleavened bread; and fire sprang up from the rock and consumed the meat and the unleavened bread. Then the angel of the Lord vanished from his sight.*

6. **God commands Gideon to tear down the altars to Baal that his father had erected and to erect an altar to the Lord in their place (Judg. 6:28–32).**

7. **Shortly afterward, many nations gather together to wipe out the Israelites.**

Judges 6:33–35: *Then all the Midianites and the Amalekites and the sons of the east assembled themselves; and they crossed over and camped in the valley of Jezreel [just north of Gideon's Spring]. 34 So the Spirit of the Lord came upon Gideon; and he blew a trumpet, and the Abiezrites were called together to follow him. 35 He sent messengers throughout Manasseh, and they also were called together to follow him; and he sent messengers to Asher, Zebulun, and Naphtali, and they came up to meet them.*

- The Midianites were the descendants of Midian and therefore, children of Abraham. They settled in "the land of the east." When Moses fled the wrath of Pharaoh, he traveled to Midian (Ex. 2:15). There, Moses met and married his wife, Zipporah, and served his father-in-law, Jethro, as a shepherd for 40 years.

- The Amalekites were the first ones to attack the Israelites upon their exodus from Egypt. Genesis 36 refers to the descendants of Amalek, the son of Eliphaz and grandson of Esau, as Amalekites. So, the Amalekites were somehow related to, but distinct from, the Edomites.

8. **As a result of the nations who had gathered together to wipe out the Israelites, Gideon asks for a sign from God that he will be successful. The sign of the wet and dry fleeces is used by Gideon to seek assurance of God's help (Judg. 6:36–40). However, it reveals a lack of faith in what God had said He would do.**

9. **God commands Gideon to choose 300 men for battle so that**

He gets all the glory for the victory.

Judges 7:1–7: *Then Jerubbaal [Gideon] and all the people who were with him rose early and encamped beside the **spring of Harod**. And the camp of Midian was north of them, by the hill of Moreh, in the valley. 2 The LORD said to Gideon,*  *"The people with you are too many for me to give the Midianites into their hand, lest Israel boast over me, saying, 'My own hand has saved me.' 3 Now therefore proclaim in the ears of the people, saying, 'Whoever is fearful and trembling, let him return home and hurry away from Mount Gilead.'" Then 22,000 of the people returned, and 10,000 remained. 4 And the LORD said to Gideon, "The people are still too many. Take them down to the water, and I will test them for you there, and anyone of whom I say to you, 'This one shall go with you,' shall go with you, and anyone of whom I say to you, 'This one shall not go with you,' shall not go." 5 So he brought the people down to the water. And the LORD said to Gideon, "Everyone who laps the water with his tongue, as a dog laps, you shall set by himself. Likewise, everyone who kneels down to drink." 6 And the number of those who lapped, putting their hands to their mouths, was 300 men, but all the rest of the people knelt down to drink water. 7 And the LORD said to Gideon, "With the 300 men who lapped I will save you and give the Midianites into your hand, and let all the others go every man to his home."*

It's believed God chose those who lapped like dogs because they were less civilized. This would give God even more glory for the victory.

10. The size of the opposing army was enormous.

Judges 7:12: *Now the Midianites and the Amalekites and all the sons of the east were lying in the valley as numerous as locusts; and their camels were without number, as numerous as the sand on the seashore.*

11. **God allows Gideon to visit the camp of the opposing army to be assured of victory.**

    Judges 7:13–14: *When Gideon came, behold, a man was relating a dream to his friend. And he said, "Behold, I had a dream; a loaf of barley bread was tumbling into the camp of Midian, and it came to the tent and struck it so that it fell, and turned it upside down so that the tent lay flat." 14 His friend replied, "This is nothing less than the sword of Gideon the son of Joash, a man of Israel; God has given Midian and all the camp into his hand."*

12. **God delivers the Midianites and Amalekites into the hands of the Israelites.**

    Judges 7:15–25: *As soon as Gideon heard the telling of the dream and its interpretation, he worshiped. And he returned to the camp of Israel and said, "Arise, for the LORD has given the host of Midian into your hand." 16 And he divided the 300 men into three companies and put trumpets into the hands of all of them and empty jars, with torches inside the jars. 17 And he said to them, "Look at me, and do likewise. When I come to the outskirts of the camp, do as I do. 18 When I blow the trumpet, I and all who are with me, then blow the trumpets also on every side of all the camp and shout, 'For the LORD and for Gideon.'" 9 So Gideon and the hundred men who were with him came to the outskirts of the camp at the beginning of the middle watch, when they had just set the watch. And they blew the trumpets and smashed the jars that were in their hands. 20 Then the three companies blew the trumpets and broke the jars. They held in their left hands the torches, and in their right hands the trumpets to blow. And they cried out, "A sword for the LORD and for Gideon!" 21 Every man stood in his place around the camp, and all the army ran. They cried out and fled. 22 When they blew the 300 trumpets, the LORD set every man's sword against his comrade and against all the army. And the army fled as far as Beth-shittah toward Zererah, as far as the border of Abel-meholah,*

Field by Gideon's Spring

by Tabbath [cities by the Jordan River directly east]. 23 And the men of Israel were called out from Naphtali and from Asher and from all Manasseh, and they pursued after Midian. 24 Gideon sent messengers throughout all the hill country of Ephraim, saying, "Come down against the Midianites and capture the waters against them, as far as Beth-barah, and also the Jordan." So all the men of Ephraim were called out, and they captured the waters as far as Beth-barah, and also the Jordan. 25 And they captured the two princes of Midian, Oreb and Zeeb. They killed Oreb at the rock of Oreb, and Zeeb they killed at the winepress of Zeeb. Then they pursued Midian, and they brought the heads of Oreb and Zeeb to Gideon across the Jordan.

Faith Lesson from Gideon's Spring

1. God often puts us in difficult situations so He gets all the glory when He helps us with our problems.
2. We, like the Israelites, can worship idols as well. An idol is anything that distracts us from our time and attention on God. What is distracting you away from God at this time in your life?
3. We should look at the size of our God rather than the size of our difficulties.
4. God delights in our faith but is grieved by our lack of it.
5. God chooses the weak things to show His glory.

   1 Cor. 1:27–29: *But God has chosen the foolish things of the world to shame the wise, and God has chosen the weak things of the world to shame the things which are strong, 28 and the base things of the world and the despised God has chosen, the things that are not, so that He may nullify the things that are, 29* ***so that no man may boast before*** *God*.

6. Even if you have weaknesses, God can use you if you trust and follow Him.

Journal/Notes:

Hazor

Location

1. Hazor is about 10 miles (16 km.) due north of the Sea of Galilee and just to the east of Hwy. 90.
2. It was on one of the most important travel routes called the "Via Maris," which linked Africa and Egypt with Europe and Asia.
3. It was the largest and most strategic city in northern Galilee due to its size and location.

Historical Background

1. Hazor was one of the most important cities of the Canaanites and was the head of all the northern kingdoms (Josh. 11:10).
2. It was 10 times the size of Jerusalem and totaled 200 acres (81 hectares, 200 football fields) in size.
3. The upper part of the tel is around 30 acres (12 hectares), and the lower part is around 170 acres (69 hectares).
4. What we see today of Hazor is 1/8 the size of what it once was.
5. To the north lies most of the city, which is now a farm field.
6. It's the largest tel in Israel.
7. It's also believed to have been the largest city in ancient Canaan.
8. It was one of three major cities of defense in Israel (Gezer, to the south, Megiddo, in the middle of the country, and Hazor, in the north). All three cities were on the Via Maris.
9. Hazor rivaled Nineveh in size and importance.
10. Hazor is mentioned 19 times in the Bible.

Places of Interest

1. Parking

Northern Israel Sites

2. Israelite Walls
3. Lower City
4. Temple Tombs
5. Northern Walls
6. Canaanite Temple/Palace
7. Solomon's Walls and Gate (archaeologists have uncovered a six-chambered gate at Hazor, which is nearly identical in size and design to the gates at Megiddo and Gezer).
8. Ash Layer in the Canaanite Palace.
9. Canaanite Altar
10. Water System (a century after Solomon's time, the Israelites built a massive shaft 131 ft. (40 m.) deep into the tel, reaching the water table below).
11. Citadel
12. Rooms & Buildings
13. Canaanite passage between the upper and lower cities.

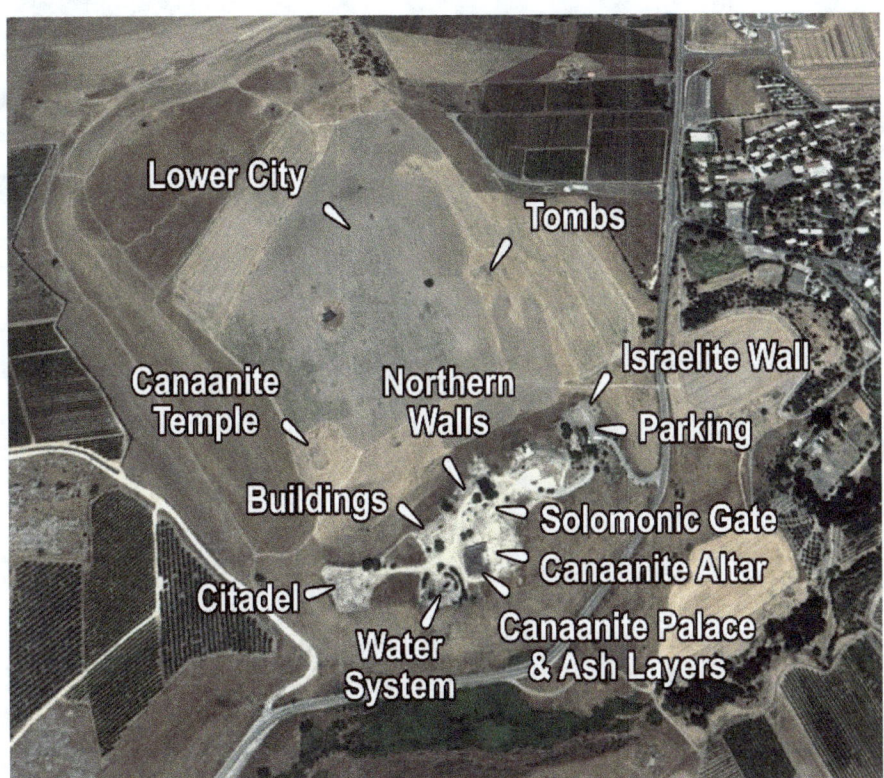

Hazor in the Bible

1. **When Jabin, king of Hazor, heard that Joshua and the Israelites had been on a conquering rampage throughout all the southern part of the land, he gathered a host of kings in the northern part of the land to unite and fight against the Israelites.**

   Joshua 11:1–5: *When Jabin, **king of Hazor**, heard of this, he sent to Jobab king of Madon, and to the king of Shimron, and to the king of Achshaph, 2 and to the kings who were in the northern hill country, and in the Arabah south of Chinneroth, and in the lowland, and in Naphoth-dor on the west, 3 to the Canaanites in the east and the west, the Amorites, the Hittites, the Perizzites, and the Jebusites in the hill country, and the Hivites under Hermon in the land of Mizpah. 4 And they came out with all their troops, a great horde, in number like the sand that is on the seashore, with very many horses and chariots. 5 And all these kings joined their forces and came and encamped together at the waters of **Merom** [3.5 miles, 5.5 km. north of Hazor] to fight against Israel.*

2. **All the unified kings and soldiers believed that with their countless armies and gods, Israel would be no match for them.**

3. **God told Joshua and the Israelites not to be afraid because He**

would be with them and deliver all these kings into their hands.

Joshua 11:6–9: *And the Lord said to Joshua, "Do not be afraid of them, for tomorrow at this time I will give over all of them, slain, to Israel. You shall hamstring their horses and burn their chariots with fire." 7 So Joshua and all his warriors came suddenly against them by the waters of **Merom** and fell upon them. 8 And the Lord gave them into the hand of Israel, who struck them and chased them as far as Great Sidon and Misrephoth-maim, and eastward as far as the Valley of Mizpeh. And they struck them until he left none remaining. 9 And Joshua did to them just as the Lord said to him: he hamstrung their horses and burned their chariots with fire.*

4. **After defeating all the armies, Joshua conquered Hazor and burned it with fire.**

   Joshua 11:10–13: *Then Joshua turned back at that time, and captured **Hazor** and struck its king with the sword; for **Hazor** formerly was the **head of all these kingdoms**. 11 They struck every person who was in it with the edge of the sword, utterly destroying them; there was no one left who breathed. **And he burned Hazor with fire**. 12 Joshua captured all the cities of these kings, and all their kings, and he struck them with the edge of the sword, and utterly destroyed them; just as Moses the servant of the Lord had commanded. 13 But none of the cities that stood on mounds did Israel burn, **except Hazor alone; that Joshua burned**.*

   Evidence of the burn marks and ash layer can be seen in the Canaanite Palace at Hazor.

5. **Hazor was later retaken and rebuilt by the Canaanites. God used the Canaanites to punish Israel for their disobedience to Him.**

Judges 4:1–3: *And the people of Israel again did what was evil in the sight of the Lord after Ehud died. 2 And the Lord sold them into the hand of Jabin [not the king's actual personal name but his title] king of Canaan, who reigned in* **Hazor**. *The commander of his army was Sisera, who lived in Harosheth-hagoyim. 3 Then the people of Israel cried out to the Lord for help, for he had 900 chariots of iron and he oppressed the people of Israel cruelly for twenty years.*

6. **God used Deborah and Barak to deliver the Israelites after they repented of their sins and cried out to Him for help.**

    Joshua 4:14–16: *And Deborah said to Barak, "Up! For this is the day in which the Lord has given Sisera into your hand. Does not the Lord go out before you?" So Barak went down from Mount Tabor with 10,000 men following him. 15 And the Lord routed Sisera and all his chariots and all his army before Barak by the edge of the sword. And Sisera got down from his chariot and fled away on foot. 16 And Barak pursued the chariots and the army to Harosheth-hagoyim, and all the army of Sisera fell by the edge of the sword; not a man was left.*

7. **Hazor later came under the control of Israel during the period of King David and Solomon, and Solomon rebuilt and fortified Hazor, along with Megiddo and Gezer.**

    1 Kings 9:15: *Now this is the account of the forced labor which King Solomon levied to build the house of the Lord, his own house, the Millo, the wall of Jerusalem,* **Hazor**, *Megiddo, and Gezer.*

8. **Jeremiah prophesied against Hazor due to the Israelites disobedience after David and Solomon's time.**

    Jeremiah 49:33: **Hazor** *will become a haunt of jackals, a desolation forever; no one will live there, nor will a son of man reside in it.*

    It's amazing that this once sought-after prime location is now

Northern Israel Sites

desolate. It shows the power of God and His proclaimed word.

9. **As a result of Israel's disobedience to God, Hazor was destroyed by Assyria in 722 BC, and the northern 10 tribes of Israel were deported.**

   2 Kings 15:29: *In the days of Pekah king of Israel, Tiglath-pileser king of Assyria came and captured Ijon, Abel-beth-maacah, Janoah, Kedesh, **Hazor**, Gilead, and Galilee, all the land of Naphtali, and he carried the people captive to Assyria.*

Faith Lesson from Hazor

1. When the Israelites obeyed God, He blessed them and made them victorious over countless kings and multitudes of soldiers.
2. When they disobeyed God, He caused them to become weak and defeated.
3. The same lesson from the Old Testament applies to us today (Rom. 15:4). When we are obedient and faithful to God, we live victoriously and receive His blessings. However, when we disobey Him, we become weak and defeated.

4. What kind of lives are we living today? Are we victorious or defeated?

Journal/Notes:

Sea of Galilee & Northern Biblical Sites Guide

Jordan River Overview

Location

1. The Jordan River begins at Mount Hermon in the northernmost part of Israel, flows into the Sea of Galilee, and then out and down to the Dead Sea.
2. The lower part of the river has the lowest elevation of any river in the world.
3. It's the border between Israel and Jordan for much of its length.
4. Today, because of the high demands of water by both Israel and Jordan, little water makes it to the Dead Sea area.

Historical Background

1. The Jordan River is mentioned over 180 times in the Bible.
2. It is the main River in Israel, supplying much of the country with water.
3. Its total winding length is about 125 miles (200 km.).
4. The meaning of "Jordan" in Hebrew is "descend." This is true of the Jordan River as it literally descends thousands of feet from its inception to its ending, and all but the beginning part is below sea level.
5. However, there's a deeper spiritual meaning to the word. In the same way we must physically descend to access the Jordan River's waters, we must descend and humble ourselves before we can ascend spiritually. This concept is seen in many of the miracles that happened in and around its shores.

Places of Interest

1. Mount Hermon – Rises to around 9,232 ft. (2,813 m.) above sea level and supplies the Jordan River with most of its water.

Northern Israel Sites

2. Hermon Stream Nature Reserve – Beginning area of the Jordan River.
3. Jordan River View – Nice viewing place where the river is wide and calm.
4. Sea of Galilee – The Jordan River flows into and out of the Sea of Galilee.
5. Yardenit Baptismal Site – Located just south of the Sea of Galilee. It's a popular place where many pilgrims get baptized in the Jordan River.
6. Adam – Place the waters of the Jordan backed up to when the Israelites crossed the river (20 miles, 32 km. above crossing).
7. Baptismal Site of Jesus – Located across from Jericho, this is the believed place where Jesus was baptized. It's also a popular place where many people get baptized today as well.
8. Crossing of the Jordan River by the Israelites – Located nearby to the Baptismal Site of Jesus.
9. Camp Gilgal
10. Jericho
11. Dead Sea

Jordan River in the Bible

1. **Abraham entered the Promised Land through the gateway of the Jordan River Valley when he first journeyed from Ur of the Chaldeans (Gen. 12:1–9).**

2. **When Abraham and Lot divided their possessions, Lot chose to settle in the lower part of the Jordan River Valley.**

   Genesis 13:10: *And Lot lifted up his eyes and saw that the **Jordan Valley** was well watered everywhere like the garden of the LORD, like the land of Egypt, in the direction of Zoar. (This was before the LORD destroyed Sodom and Gomorrah.)*

3. **Before entering the Promised Land, the Israelites camped on the east side of the Jordan River, opposite Jericho.**

   Joshua 3:1: *Then Joshua rose early in the morning, and they set out from Shittim. And they came to the **Jordan**, he and all the people of Israel, and lodged there before they passed over.*

4. **The Israelites crossed the Jordan River on dry ground as God miraculously parted the waters.**

   Joshua 3:14–17: *So when the people set out from their tents to pass over the **Jordan** with the priests bearing the ark of the covenant before the people, 15 and as soon as those bearing the ark had come as far as the **Jordan**, and the **feet of the priests** bearing the ark were dipped in the brink*

   Hermon Springs Nature Reserve (Caesarea Philippi)

   *of the water (**now the Jordan overflows all its banks throughout the time of harvest**), 16 the waters coming down from above stood and rose up in a heap very far away, at Adam [20 miles, 32 km. north], the city that is beside Zarethan, and those flowing down toward the Sea of the Arabah, the Salt Sea, were completely cut off. And the people passed over opposite Jericho. 17 Now the priests bearing the ark of the covenant of the Lord stood firmly on dry ground **in the midst of the Jordan**, and all Israel was passing over on dry ground until all the nation finished passing over the **Jordan**.*

5. **Naaman, the Leper, was healed in the Jordan River by the Prophet Elisha.**

   2 Kings 5:10–14: *And Elisha sent a messenger to him, saying, "Go and wash in the **Jordan** seven times, and your flesh shall be restored, and you shall be clean." 11 But Naaman was angry and went away, saying, "Behold, I thought that he would surely come out to me and stand and call upon the name of the LORD his God, and wave his hand over the place and cure the leper. 12 Are not Abana and Pharpar, the rivers of Damascus, better than all the waters of Israel? Could I not wash in them and be clean?" So he turned and went away in a rage. 13 But his servants came near and said to him, "My father, it is a great word the prophet has spoken to you; will you not do it? Has he actually said to you, 'Wash, and be clean?'" 14 So he went down and dipped himself seven times in the **Jordan**, according to the word of the man of God, and his flesh was restored like the flesh of a little child, and he was clean.*

   Jordan River north of the Sea of Galilee

6. **Elijah parted the waters of the Jordan with his cloak.**

   2 Kings 2:6–8: *Then Elijah said to him, "Please stay here, for the Lord has sent me to the Jordan." But he said, "As the Lord lives, and as you yourself live, I will not leave you." So the two of them went on. 7 Fifty men of the sons of the prophets also went and stood at some distance from them, as they both were standing by the **Jordan**. 8 Then Elijah took his cloak and rolled it up and struck the water, and the water was parted to the one side and to the other, till the two of them could go over on dry ground.*

7. **Elisha made the head of an ax float at the Jordan River.**

   2 Kings 6:1–7: *Now the sons of the prophets said to Elisha, "See, the place where we dwell under your charge is too small for us. 2 Let us go to the **Jordan** and each of us get there a log, and let us make a*

place for us to dwell there." And he answered, "Go." 3 Then one of them said, "Be pleased to go with your servants." And he answered, "I will go." 4 So he went with them. And when they came to the **Jordan**, *they cut down trees. 5 But as one was felling a log, his axe head fell into the water, and he cried out, "Alas, my master! It was borrowed." 6 Then the man of God said, "Where did it fall?" When he showed him the place, he cut off a stick and threw it in there and made the iron float. 7 And he said, "Take it up." So he reached out his hand and took it.*

8. **John the Baptist baptized many people in the Jordan River.**

   Matthew 3:5–6: *Then Jerusalem and all Judea and all the region about the Jordan were going out to him, 6 and they were baptized by him in the* **river Jordan**, *confessing their sins.*

9. **Jesus was baptized in the Jordan River by John the Baptist.**

   Matthew 3:13–17: *Then Jesus came from Galilee to the* **Jordan** *to John, to be baptized by him. 14 John would have prevented him, saying, "I need to be baptized by you, and do you come to me?" 15 But Jesus answered him, "Let it be so now, for thus it is fitting for us to fulfill all righteousness." Then he consented. 16 And when Jesus was baptized, immediately he went up from the water, and*

Yardenit Baptismal Site

behold, the heavens were opened to him, and he saw the Spirit of God descending like a dove and coming to rest on him; 17 and behold, a voice from heaven said, "This is my beloved Son, with whom I am well pleased."

10. **The disciples of Jesus baptized many people in the Jordan River.**

    John 4:1–3: *Now when Jesus learned that the Pharisees had heard that Jesus was making and baptizing more disciples than John 2 (although Jesus himself did not baptize, but only his disciples), 3 he left Judea and departed again for Galilee.*

Faith Lesson from the Jordan River

1. The Jordan River represented life and vitality to the Israelites. They were desert people, and water was their life. Therefore, Christ used this concept to teach them that in the same way water was vital for their physical lives, He was vital for their spiritual lives as well. Do we realize the importance of a close relationship with Christ in order to have spiritual life and vitality?

2. The meaning of Jordan means "descend." In a spiritual sense, are we humble before God and submissive to Him in order to grow spiritually?

3. The Israelites crossed the Jordan River on dry ground. In so doing, God reminded them of the miracle of crossing the Red Sea after their exodus from Egypt. Often, God will repeat miracles to show His faithfulness. What things has God done repeatedly to show His faithfulness to us?

Baptismal Site of Jesus

4. Naaman, the leper, had his own idea of how God should operate. Do we often have our own ideas as well as to how we think God should do things?

5. Baptism played a major role in the ministries of John the Baptist, Jesus, and his disciples. It was a baptism of repentance. What is our view of baptism today, and how important is it to us and our ministries?

Journal/Notes:

Sea of Galilee & Northern Biblical Sites Guide

Megiddo: Valley of Armageddon

Location

1. Tel Megiddo is about 15 miles (26 km.) east of the Mediterranean Ocean and about 25 miles (40 km.) southwest of the Sea of Galilee.
2. Megiddo lay at the juncture of several key routes (the main route is called the Via Maris) which linked Africa to Asia and Europe. For this reason, any country that rose to world power had to control Megiddo due to its strategic location.
3. More battles have been fought in this location than any other place in the entire world.
4. The name Armageddon is derived from "Har-Megiddo," which is translated, "Armageddon." Har means hill, and Megeddon is the place. When these words are joined together, it is Armageddon.
5. Today, this place is called Megiddo in English. It's located in the most fertile valley in Israel called the Jezreel Valley.
6. It is a "Tel," which is made up of layer upon layer of different civilizations that make up an artificial hill.
7. Tel Megiddo is made up of 25–26 layers of civilizations.
8. Today, you can see a busy highway right beside Tel Megiddo that uses the same ancient travel route that has been used for 6,000 years.
9. One of the Pharaohs, Thutmose the III, said conquering Megiddo was like conquering a thousand cities.

Historical Background

1. 4000 BC: Early Settlements.
2. 2000 BC: Massive city walls were built.

3. 1800 BC: A Canaanite gate was constructed on the north side.
4. 1500 BC: The gate and walls were rebuilt.
5. 1468 BC: The city rebelled against the Egyptians with other Canaanite cities and was conquered by Thutmose III after a great battle and a 7-month siege.
6. 960 BC: New gate and walls were built by the Israelites under Solomon's command.
7. 945 BC: Pharaoh Shishak conquered the city (1 Kings 14:25). A fragment of a tablet with Pharaoh Shishak's name was found here.
8. 850 BC: King Ahab fortified Megiddo and dug a water tunnel to access water within the city walls.
9. 732 BC: The city was captured by the Assyrian King Tiglath-Pileser III. Megiddo became the capital of the Assyrian province of the Galilee.

Canaanite Gates

10. 650 BC: Battle between the Egyptian Army and the Kingdom of Judah (King Josiah died in this battle).
11. 609 BC: The Egyptians replaced the Assyrians.
12. 300 BC: The city was abandoned, and the Tel was left in ruins.
13. 1918 AD: Battles between the British and the Turks in WWI. Britain gained control over Israel.
14. 1948 AD: Britain granted independence to Israel.
15. 1949 AD: Kibbutz Megiddo was established on the south side of Tel Megiddo.

Places of Interest

1. Canaanite Gate with 4 Towers
2. Canaanite Palace
3. Israelite Gate with 6 Towers

4. Northern Horse Stables
5. Northern Palace
6. Large cut through the tel was carried out between 1903 and 1905 by Gottlieb Schumacher for the German Society for Oriental Research.
7. Canaanite Temple and Altar – Place of animal sacrifice, and possibly children, to false gods.
8. Burial Chamber
9. Public Structure
10. Four-room House
11. Grain Silo
12. Southern Palace
13. Southern Horse Stables
14. Assyrian City
15. Water tunnel dug by King Ahab to protect the water source from enemies.
16. View of the Jezreel Valley (Valley of Armageddon).

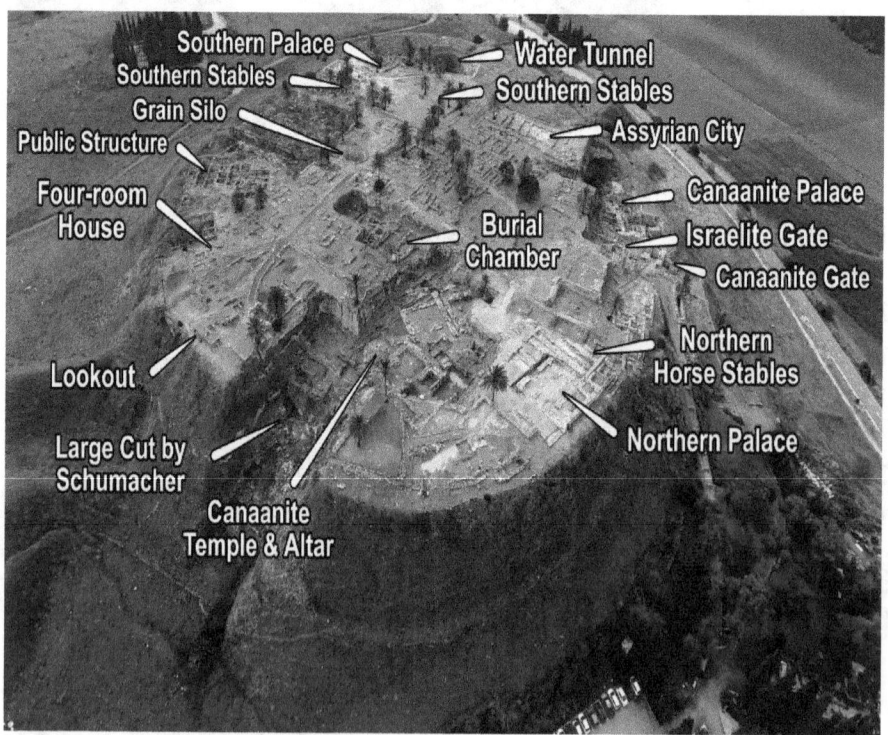

Northern Israel Sites

Tel Megiddo in the Bible

1. **King Solomon fortified Megiddo and used it for a fort of protection.**

   1 Kings 9:15: *Now this is the account of the forced labor which King Solomon levied to build the house of the Lord, his own house, the Millo, the wall of Jerusalem, Hazor, **Megiddo**, and Gezer.*

2. **A monumental battle will be fought here and in Jerusalem at the end of the Great Tribulation Period.**

   Revelation 16:1–21: *Then I heard a loud voice from the temple telling the seven angels, "Go and pour out on the earth the **seven bowls of the wrath of God**." 2 So the **first angel** went and poured*

   Jezreel Valley (Armageddon) from Megiddo

   *out his bowl on the earth, and harmful and painful sores came upon the people who bore the mark of the beast and worshiped its image. 3 The **second angel** poured out his bowl into the sea, and it became like the blood of a corpse, and every living thing died that was in the sea. 4 The **third angel** poured out his bowl into the rivers and the springs of water, and they became blood. 5 And I heard the angel in charge of the waters say, "Just are you, O Holy One, who is and who was, for you brought these judgments. 6 For they have shed the blood of saints and prophets, and you have given them blood to drink. It is what they deserve!" 7 And I heard the altar saying, "Yes, Lord God the Almighty, true and just are your judgments!" 8 The **fourth angel** poured out his bowl on the sun, and it was allowed to scorch people with fire. 9 They were scorched by the fierce heat, and they cursed the name of God who had power over these plagues. They did not repent and give him glory. 10 The **fifth angel** poured out his bowl on the throne of the beast, and its kingdom was plunged into darkness. People gnawed their tongues in anguish 11 and cursed the God of heaven for their pain and sores. They did not* repent of their deeds. 12 The **sixth angel** poured out his bowl on the great river Euphrates, and its water was dried up, to prepare the way for the kings from the east. 13 And I saw, coming out of the mouth of the dragon and out of the mouth of the beast and out of the mouth of the false prophet, three unclean spirits like frogs. 14 For they are demonic spirits, performing signs, who go abroad to the kings of the whole world, to assemble them for battle on the great day of God the Almighty. 15 ("Behold, I am coming like a thief! Blessed is the one who stays awake, keeping his garments on, that he may not go about naked and be seen exposed!") 16 And they assembled them at the place that in Hebrew is called **Armageddon**. 17 The **seventh angel** poured out his bowl into the air, and a loud voice came out of the temple, from the throne, saying, "It is done!" 18 And there were flashes of lightning, rumblings, peals of thunder, and a great earthquake such as there had never been since man was on the earth, so great was

Canaanite Altar

that earthquake. 19 The great city was split into three parts, and the cities of the nations fell, and God remembered Babylon the great, to make her drain the cup of the wine of the fury of his wrath. 20 And every island fled away, and no mountains were to be found. 21 And great hailstones, about one hundred pounds each, fell from heaven on people; and they cursed God for the plague of the hail, because the plague was so severe.

3. **The harvest of the earth in God's winepress of wrath in Jerusalem.**

   Revelation 14:14–20: *Then I looked, and behold, a white cloud, and seated on the cloud one like a son of man, with a golden crown on his head, and a sharp sickle in his hand. 15 And another angel came out of the temple, calling with a loud voice to him who sat on the cloud, "Put in your sickle, and reap, for the hour to reap has come, for the harvest of the earth is fully ripe." 16 So he who sat on the cloud swung his sickle across the earth, and the earth was reaped. 17 Then another angel came out of the temple in heaven, and he too had a sharp sickle. 18 And another angel came out from the altar, the angel who has authority over the fire, and he called with a loud voice to the one who had the sharp sickle, "Put in your sickle and gather the clusters from the vine of the earth, for its grapes are ripe." 19 So the angel swung his sickle across the earth and gathered the grape harvest of the earth and threw it into the great winepress of the wrath of God. 20 And the winepress was trodden* **outside the city** *[Jerusalem], and blood flowed from the winepress, as high as a horse's bridle, for 1,600 stadia [180 miles, 300 km.].*

Matthew 25:31–34: *When the Son of Man comes in his glory, and all the angels with him, then he will sit on his glorious throne. 32 Before him will be gathered all the nations, and he will separate people one from another as a shepherd separates the sheep from the goats. 33 And he will place the sheep on his right, but the goats on the left. 34 Then the King will say to those on his right, "Come, you who are blessed by my Father, inherit the kingdom prepared for you from the foundation of the world."*

Matthew 25:46: *And these will go away into eternal punishment, but the righteous into eternal life.*

Faith Lesson from Megiddo

1. Part of the last battle of Armageddon will be fought in Megiddo and the other part in Jerusalem. The war seems to happen simultaneously.
2. This battle will take place at the end of the Great Tribulation

Period.

3. Scripture says that unless these days were shortened, no life would survive.
4. The Tribulation Period will be a time when God pours out His wrath on a world that has rejected Him inspite of all He has done for them.
5. Where will I be at this battle? Will I be fighting with Christ or against Him?
6. Water was the source of life for all cities in ancient days. These cities could be conquered when their enemies cut off their water supply.

7. God's Word is our water source of life. Our enemy, Satan, can defeat us by cutting off our intake of God's Word. When he can do this, he can conquer us. To stand against Satan and his attacks, am I daily drinking abundantly from the water source of God's Word?

Journal/Notes:

Northern Israel Sites

Mount Carmel

Location

1. The place marking the great showdown between Elijah and the false prophets is known as Deir Al-Mukhraqa Carmelite Monastery.
2. Mount Carmel is located about 9 miles (15 km.) east of the Mediterranean Sea in the Carmel Mountain Range, which is in the northern part of Israel. It's also about 28 miles (44 km.) southwest of the Sea of Galilee.
3. Mount Carmel was a High Place of worship to the false god of Baal and Asherah during the period of Judges, 1 & 2 Samuel, and 1 & 2 Kings.
4. It has a spectacular view of the Jezreel Valley, which is also known as the Valley of Armageddon. Armageddon is where part of the last battle on earth takes place at the end of the Great Tribulation Period.
5. From Mount Carmel, Nazareth and Cana can be seen to the northeast.

Historical Background

1. The great showdown between the Prophet Elijah and the 850 prophets of Baal and Asherah began around 100 years earlier when King Solomon sowed the seeds that would destroy Israel morally.
2. Against God's clear commandments to the Israelites, Solomon married many foreign wives.
3. These foreign wives worshiped false gods, and in order to honor them, Solomon built high places of worship all over Israel where these false gods could be worshiped. 1 Kings 11 recounts this

tragic reality.

4. As a result, the worship of false gods became rampant in the land.
5. Because of the worship of false gods, God pronounced judgment on the nation of Israel, and it was divided into two kingdoms after Solomon's death.
6. Rehoboam, one of Solomon's sons, took the Southern Kingdom of Judah, which consisted of 2 tribes, and Jeroboam, one of Solomon's officials, took the Northern Kingdom, which consisted of 10 tribes.

Mount Carmel

7. Because Jeroboam was afraid many of his people would defect to Rehoboam's kingdom by going to Jerusalem to worship God in the temple there, he introduced false gods into the northern tribes of Israel.
8. Jeroboam erected two golden calf altars at Bethel and Dan for his people to worship at instead of going to the temple in Jerusalem. He told his people that these golden calves were the gods who led them out of Egypt.
9. Several kings later, King Ahab, king of the Northern Kingdom, married a foreign wife named Jezebel, who worshiped the false gods of Baal (a male god) and Asherah (a female god). Jezebel promoted worship to these false gods by employing countless prophets of Baal and Asherah. She even supported them financially and fed them at her royal table.
10. Mt. Carmel was one of the key high places in Israel where the people worshiped Baal and Asherah.
11. Baal and Asherah were the gods of the weather. It was for this reason God sent a drought and then later sent rain. By doing so, He showed He was the true God of the weather and everything else. Baal worship was originally from the Canaanite nations God drove out because of their extreme wickedness.

Northern Israel Sites

Places of Interest

1. Mt. Carmel
2. Kishon Stream
3. Jezreel Valley
4. Tel Jezreel
5. Mediterranean Sea

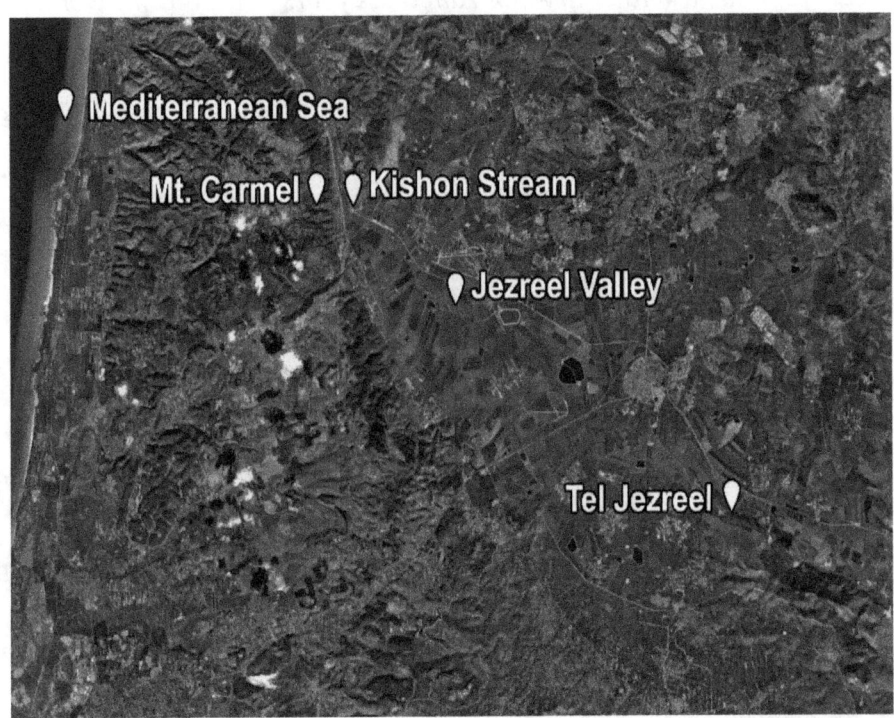

Mount Carmel in the Bible

1. **The showdown between Elijah and the false prophets took place during the reign of Ahab, King of Israel.**

   1 Kings 16:29–33: *In the thirty-eighth year of Asa king of Judah, Ahab the son of Omri began to reign over Israel, and Ahab the son of Omri reigned over Israel in Samaria twenty-two years. 30 And Ahab the son of Omri did evil in the sight of the LORD, more than all who were before him. 31 And as if it had been a light thing for him to walk in the sins of Jeroboam the son of Nebat, he took for his wife Jezebel, the daughter of Ethbaal king of the Sidonians, and went and served Baal and worshiped him. 32 He erected an altar for Baal in*

the house of Baal, which he built in Samaria. 33 And Ahab made an Asherah. Ahab did more to provoke the LORD, the God of Israel, to anger than all the kings of Israel who were before him.

2. **Because of Ahab's great sin, God sent a severe drought over all the land.**

   1 Kings 17:1: *Now Elijah the Tishbite, of Tishbe in Gilead, said to Ahab, "As the LORD, the God of Israel, lives, before whom I stand, there shall be neither dew nor rain these years, except by my word."*

3. **After these 3 years had ended, Elijah confronts Ahab and promises God will send rain.**

   1 Kings 18:1–2: *After many days the word of the LORD came to Elijah, in the third year, saying, "Go, show yourself to Ahab, and I will send rain upon the earth." 2 So Elijah went to show himself to Ahab. Now the famine was severe in Samaria.*

   Mount Carmel

   1 Kings 18:17–19: *When Ahab saw Elijah, Ahab said to him, "Is it you, you troubler of Israel?" 18 And he answered, "I have not troubled Israel, but you have, and your father's house, because you have abandoned the commandments of the Lord and followed the Baals. 19 Now, therefore, send and gather all Israel to me at Mount Carmel, and the 450 prophets of Baal and the 400 prophets of Asherah, who eat at Jezebel's table."*

4. **The great gathering of all the people.**

   1 Kings 18:20–21: *So Ahab sent to all the people of Israel and gathered the prophets together at Mount Carmel. 21 And Elijah came near to all the people and said, "How long will you go limping between two different opinions? If the Lord is God, follow him; but if Baal, then follow him." And the people did not answer him a word.*

5. **The great contest between Elijah and the 850 prophets of Baal and Asherah.**

   1 Kings 18:22–24: *Then Elijah said to the people, "I, even I only, am left a prophet of the Lord, but Baal's prophets are 450 men. 23 Let two bulls be given to us, and let them choose one bull for themselves and cut it in pieces and lay it on the wood, but put no fire to it. And I will prepare the other bull and lay it on the wood and put no fire to it. 24 And you call upon the name of your god, and I will call upon the name of the Lord, and the God who answers by fire, he is God." And all the people answered, "It is well spoken."*

6. **The false prophets of Baal and Asherah go first.**

   1 Kings 18:25–29: *Then Elijah said to the prophets of Baal, "Choose for yourselves one bull and prepare it first, for you are many, and call upon the name of your god, but put no fire to it." 26 And they took the bull that was given them, and they prepared it and called upon the name of Baal from morning until noon, saying, "O Baal, answer us!" But there was no voice, and no one answered. And they limped around the altar that they had made. 27 And at noon Elijah mocked them, saying, "Cry aloud, for he is a god. Either he is musing, or he is relieving himself, or he is on a journey, or perhaps he is asleep and must be awakened." 28 And they cried aloud and cut themselves after their custom with swords and lances, until the blood gushed out upon them. 29 And as midday passed, they raved on until the time of the offering of the oblation [evening sacrifice], but there was no voice. No one answered; no one paid attention.*

7. **Elijah takes his turn.**

   1 Kings 18:30–35: *Then Elijah said to all the people, "Come near to me." And all the people came near to him. And he repaired the altar of the Lord that had been thrown down. 31 Elijah took twelve stones, according to the number of the tribes of the sons of Jacob, to whom*

the word of the Lord came, saying, "Israel shall be your name," 32 and with the stones he built an altar in the name of the Lord. And he made a trench about the altar, as great as would contain two seahs [about 1 foot deep by 1 foot wide] of seed. 33 And he put the wood in order and cut the bull in pieces and laid it on the wood. And he said,

"Fill four jars with water and pour it on the burnt offering and on the wood." 34 And he said, "Do it a second time." And they did it a second time. And he said, "Do it a third time." And they did it a third time. 35 And the water ran around the altar and filled the trench also with water.

8. **God miraculously answers.**

   1 Kings 18:36–39: *And at the time of the offering of the oblation, Elijah the prophet came near and said, "O Lord, God of Abraham, Isaac, and Israel, let it be known this day that you are God in Israel, and that I am your servant, and that I have done all these things at your word. 37 Answer me, O Lord, answer me, that this people may know that you, O Lord, are God, and that you have turned their hearts back." 38 Then the fire of the Lord fell and consumed the burnt offering and the wood and the stones and the dust, and licked up the water that was in the trench. 39 And when all the people saw it, they fell on their faces and said, "The Lord, he is God; the Lord, he is God."*

9. **Elijah then slaughters the false prophets below Mount Carmen at the Kishon Stream.**

   1 Kings 18:40: *And Elijah said to them, "Seize the prophets of Baal; let not one of them escape." And they seized them. And Elijah brought them down to the brook Kishon and slaughtered them there.*

Northern Israel Sites

10. Afterward, God sent a massive rainstorm which brought a deluge of rain to Israel and ended the drought.

1 Kings 18:41–46: *And Elijah said to Ahab, "Go up, eat and drink, for there is a sound of the rushing of rain." 42 So Ahab went up to eat and to drink. And Elijah went up to the top of Mount Carmel. And he bowed himself down on the earth and put his face between his knees. 43 And he said to his servant, "Go up now, look toward the sea." And he went up and looked and said, "There is nothing." And he said, "Go again," seven times. 44 And at the seventh time he said, "Behold, a little cloud like a man's hand is rising from the sea." And he said, "Go up, say to Ahab, 'Prepare your chariot and go down, lest the rain stop you.'" 45 And in a little while, the heavens grew black with clouds and wind, and there was a great rain. And Ahab rode and went to Jezreel. 46 And the hand of the Lord was on Elijah, and he gathered up his garment and ran before Ahab to the entrance of Jezreel.*

Statue of Elijah at Mount Carmel

Jezreel is about 15 miles (24 km.) directly east of Mount Carmel.

11. Unfortunately, this great miracle and spiritual revival didn't last long. Soon afterward, the country fell back into the worship of false gods and idols.

Faith Lesson from Mount Carmel

1. Do we fall away easily from the Lord and neglect Him?
2. Does spiritual revival in our lives rapidly fade?
3. Are we undisciplined in our time with God and fail to read His Word and grow in Him?
4. Have we witnessed miracles in our lives where we know that God is real and that He has shown Himself powerful to us?

5. After seeing miracles and experiencing God's help, do we forget and fall away from God afterward?

6. Are we steadfast in our relationship with God, or are we like the Israelites who were unstable with big ups and downs?

Viewing platform

7. Are we in need of coming back to God today and getting right with Him once again?

Journal/Notes:

Northern Israel Sites

Mount Tabor

Location

1. Mount Tabor, rising like a dome-like mountain from the Plain of Jezreel, is the place where Christian tradition places the transfiguration of Jesus.
2. It's about 11 miles (15 km.) southwest of the Sea of Galilee and about 5 miles (8 km.) east of Nazareth.
3. Mount Tabor stands some 1,500 ft. (457 m.) above the Jezreel Valley plain in Lower Galilee.
4. It held a strategic position at the junction of several trade routes. For this reason, many battles have been fought around it.
5. It's mentioned as one of the key mountains in Scripture: *The north and the south, you have created them;* **Tabor** *and Hermon joyously praise your name* (Ps. 89:12).

Historical Background

1. In the Old Testament, Mount Tabor is described as a sacred mountain and a place for worship. However, it's not mentioned by name in the New Testament.
2. Throughout its history, it has been a place where mankind has sought contact with the divine.
3. It also served as an important fortress during the Old Testament, Greek, Roman, and Crusader times.
4. It is best known as the believed place where the transfiguration of Christ took place, an event in the Gospels in which Jesus is transfigured upon an unnamed mountain and speaks with Moses and Elijah as described in Matthew 17:1–9; Mark 9:2–8; and Luke 9:28–36.

5. Christian tradition in the early centuries named Mount Tabor as the place of the transfiguration of Christ. This location is cited in early apocryphal writings and was accepted by the Syriac and Byzantine churches.
6. The earliest identification of the Mount of Transfiguration as Mount Tabor is by Origen in the 3rd century.
7. During the Byzantine period, due to the importance of Mount Tabor in Christian tradition, it became a pilgrimage site from the 4th century and onward. According to descriptions of the pilgrims visiting this site during the 6th century, there were three churches that resided on the top of Mount Tabor.

Franciscan Basilica of the Transformation

8. Some biblical scholars today now question this tradition. These scholars see the much higher Mount Hermon as a more likely location as it was closer to Caesarea Philippi, where Peter's confession of Christ took place.
9. However, there is great value in considering the 2,000-year-old traditions of history at this site.
10. Scripture says that the transfiguration of Christ took place 6 days after Peter's confession of Christ in Caesarea Philippi. Mount Tabor is only about 40 miles (65 km.) south of Caesarea Philippi, which could easily have been reached in 6 days.
11. It's really not important where this event happened but that it did happen.
12. Today, there are two main churches and monasteries on top of Mount Tabor, marking the event of the transfiguration of Christ. They include the Franciscan Basilica of the Transfiguration and St. Elias Greek Orthodox Church.

Northern Israel Sites

Places of Interest

1. Franciscan Basilica of the Transfiguration – Main church that is visited and sits at the highest part of Mount Tabor. This church, which is part of a Franciscan monastery complex, was completed in 1924. It was built on the ruins of an ancient 4th to 6th-century Byzantine church and a 12th-century church of the Crusader Kingdom period.
2. St. Elias Greek Orthodox Church – Located on the northern side of Mount Tabor (named after the Prophet Elijah).
3. Tower & Walls
4. Other ancient structures, chapels, cisterns, and quarries.
5. Descentibus Chapel
6. Melchizedek Chapel
7. Jezreel Valley

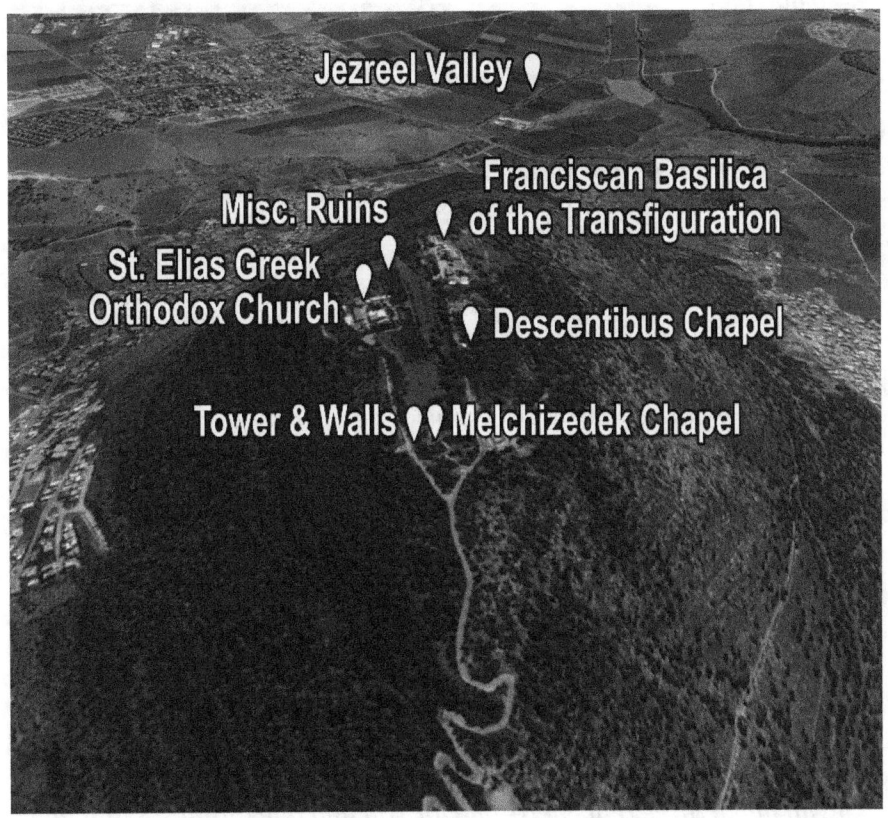

Mount Tabor in the Bible

1. **Mount Tabor is mentioned 12 times in Scripture.**
2. **It's first mentioned in Joshua 19:22 as a border between the 3 tribes of Zebulun, Issachar, and Naphtali. The mountain's prominence is due to its strategic location at the junction of the Galilee's north-south route, along with the east-west highway of the Jezreel Valley.**
3. **According to Judges chapter 4, Hazor was the seat of Jabin, the king of Canaan. His military commander, Sisera, led a Canaanite army against the Israelites. Deborah, the Jewish prophetess, summoned Barak of the tribe of Naphtali and gave him the following command.**

   *Judges 4:14–16: And Deborah said to Barak, "Up! For this is the day in which the Lord has given Sisera into your hand. Does not the Lord go out before you?" So, Barak went down from **Mount Tabor** with 10,000 men following him. 15 And the Lord routed Sisera and all his chariots and all his army before Barak by the edge of the sword.*

   And Sisera got down from his chariot and fled away on foot. 16 And Barak pursued the chariots and the army to Harosheth-hagoyim, and all the army of Sisera fell by the edge of the sword; not a man was left.

4. **Transfiguration of Christ.**

   Matthew 17:1–13: And after six days Jesus took with him Peter and James, and John, his brother, and led them up a high mountain by themselves. 2 And he was transfigured before them, and his face shone like the sun, and his clothes became white as light. 3 And behold, there appeared to them Moses and Elijah, talking with him. 4 And Peter said to Jesus, "Lord, it is good that we are here. If you wish, I will make three tents here, one for you and one for Moses and one for Elijah." 5 He was still speaking when, behold, a bright cloud overshadowed them, and a voice from the cloud said, "This is my beloved Son, with whom I am well pleased; listen to him." 6 When the disciples heard this, they fell on their faces and were terrified. 7 But Jesus came and touched them, saying, "Rise, and have no fear." 8 And when they lifted up their eyes, they saw no one but Jesus only. 9 And as they were coming down the mountain, Jesus commanded them, "Tell no one the vision, until the Son of Man is raised from the dead." 10 And the disciples asked him, "Then why do the scribes say that first Elijah must come?" 11 He answered, "Elijah does come, and he will restore all things. 12 But I tell you that Elijah has already come, and they did not recognize him, but did to him whatever they pleased. So also, the Son of Man will certainly suffer at their hands." 13 Then the disciples understood that he was speaking to them of John the Baptist.

5. **After descending Mount Tabor, Christ healed a man and used Mount Tabor as an example of faith.**

   Matthew 17:14–20: *And when they came to the crowd, a man came up to him and, kneeling before him, 15 said, "Lord, have mercy on my son, for he has seizures and he suffers terribly. For often he falls into the fire, and often into the water. 16 And I brought him to your*

   Melchizedek Chapel

   disciples, and they could not heal him." 17 And Jesus answered, "O faithless and twisted generation, how long am I to be with you? How long am I to bear with you? Bring him here to me." 18 And Jesus rebuked the demon, and it came out of him, and the boy was healed instantly. 19 Then the disciples came to Jesus privately and said, "Why could we not cast it out?" 20 He said to them, "Because of your little faith. For truly, I say to you, if you have faith like a grain of mustard seed, you will say to **this mountain**, *'Move from here to there,' and it will move, and nothing will be impossible for you."*

Faith Lesson from Mount Tabor

1. The transfiguration of Christ is another proof that He was truly the Son of God and divine.
2. It cemented in the hearts of Peter, James, and John, who would become key leaders in the early church, that Christ was definitely the Messiah and God the Father in the flesh.
3. The Apostle Peter looked back to this landmark event of the transfiguration to speak about how sure and solid our faith in Christ and His Word is.

    1 Peter 1:16-21: *For we did not follow cleverly devised myths when we made known to you the power and coming of our Lord Jesus Christ, but we were eyewitnesses of his majesty. 17 For when he received honor and glory from God the Father, and the voice was borne to him by the Majestic Glory, "This is my beloved Son, with whom I am well pleased," 18 we ourselves heard this very voice borne from heaven, for we were with him on the holy mountain [mount of transfiguration]. 19 And we have the prophetic word more fully confirmed, to which you will do well to pay attention as to a lamp shining in a dark place, until the day dawns and the morning star rises in your hearts, 20 knowing this first of all, that no prophecy of Scripture comes from someone's own interpretation [source or wisdom]. 21 For no prophecy was ever produced by the will of man, but men spoke from God as they were carried along by the Holy Spirit.*

4. Are we anchored in our faith and unmovable?
5. Do we believe Christ was God in the flesh, and are we willing to follow Him and be His disciples?
6. Do we believe we can move spiritual mountains if we have faith in Christ?

Journal/Notes:

Northern Israel Sites

Nazareth Overview

Location

1. Nazareth is in the northern part of Israel in the Lower Galilee area.
2. It's about 15 miles (24 km.) southwest of the Sea of Galilee, about 3.5 miles (5.6 km.) southwest of Cana, and about 23 miles (37 km.) inland from the Mediterranean Sea.

Historical Background

1. Nazareth had an estimated population of around 300 people during the time of Christ.
2. It's a famous town because it's where the Angel Gabriel announced the miraculous virgin birth to Mary.
3. Nazareth is also the place where Jesus grew up.
4. It was a small farming town where everyone knew each other.
5. For some reason, Nazareth had a bad reputation.

   John 1:43–46: *The next day He purposed to go into Galilee, and He found Philip. And Jesus said to him, "Follow Me." 44 Now Philip was from Bethsaida, of the city of Andrew and Peter. 45 Philip found Nathanael and said to him, "We have found Him of whom Moses in the Law and also the Prophets wrote—Jesus of Nazareth, the son of Joseph." 46 Nathanael said to him, "**Can any good thing come out of Nazareth?**" Philip said to him, "Come and see."*

Places of Interest

1. Church of the Annunciation (also known as the Basilica of the Annunciation)
2. Mary's Well
3. Greek Catholic Church
4. Synagogue Church

5. Greek Orthodox Church of the Annunciation
6. St. Joseph's Church
7. Mensa Christi Church
8. Greek Catholic Church
9. Mount Precipice

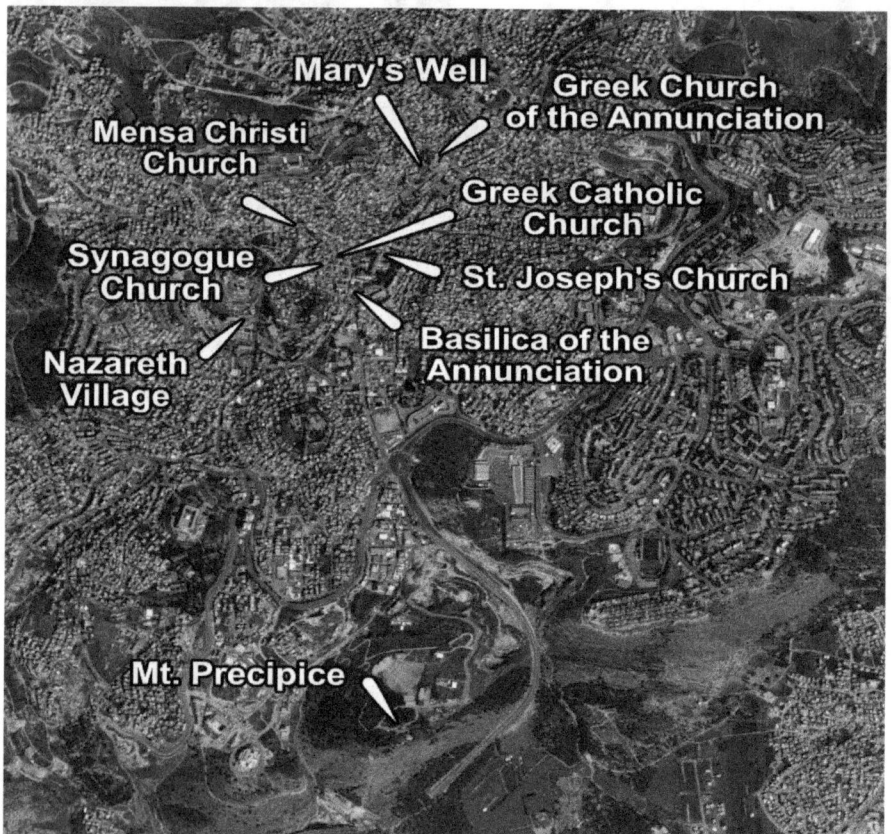

Nazareth in the Bible

1. Nazareth was the home of Joseph and Mary and the place where the angel Gabriel was sent to announce to Mary, a virgin, that she would be the mother of Christ the Messiah.
2. There have been two churches built here to commemorate this announcement. One is called the "Church of the Annunciation," and the other, the "Greek Orthodox Church of the Annunciation." The Church of the Annunciation has the most evidence of being the true site.

Luke 1:26-38: In the sixth month the angel Gabriel was sent from God to a city of Galilee named Nazareth, 27 to a virgin betrothed to a man whose name was Joseph, of the house of David. And the virgin's name was Mary. 28 And he came to her and said, "Greetings, O favored one, the Lord is with you!" 29 But she was greatly troubled at the saying,

Inside the Church of the Annunciation: Believed Home of Joseph & Mary

and tried to discern what sort of greeting this might be. 30 And the angel said to her, "Do not be afraid, Mary, for you have found favor with God. 31 And behold, you will conceive in your womb and bear a son, and you shall call his name Jesus. 32 He will be great and will be called the Son of the Most High. And the Lord God will give to him the throne of his father David, 33 and he will reign over the house of Jacob forever, and of his kingdom there will be no end." 34 And Mary said to the angel, "How will this be, since I am a virgin?" 35 And the angel answered her, "The Holy Spirit will come upon you, and the power of the Most High will overshadow you; therefore, the child to be born will be called holy—the Son of God. 36 And behold, your relative Elizabeth in her old age has also conceived a son, and this is the sixth month with her who was called barren. 37 For nothing will be impossible with God." 38 And Mary said, "Behold, I am the servant of the Lord; let it be to me according to your word." And the angel departed from her.

3. **After living in Egypt for some time after Christ's birth, His parents returned to Nazareth, where Jesus grew up.**

    Matthew 2:19-23: But when Herod died, behold, an angel of the Lord appeared in a dream to Joseph in Egypt, 20 saying, "Rise, take the child and his mother and go to the land of Israel, for those who sought the child's life are dead." 21 And he rose and took the child and his mother and went to the land of Israel. 22 But when he heard that Archelaus was reigning over Judea in place of his father Herod, he was afraid to go there, and being warned in a dream he withdrew to the district of Galilee. 23 And he went and lived in a city called **Nazareth**, that what was spoken by the prophets might be fulfilled: "He shall be called a Nazarene."

Luke 2:51–52: *And He went down with them and came to* **Nazareth**, *and He continued in subjection to them; and His mother treasured all these things in her heart. 52 And Jesus kept increasing in wisdom and stature, and in favor with God and men.*

4. **Jesus lived in Nazareth until He started His earthly ministry at the age of 30. From Nazareth, Christ relocated and set up His ministry home base in Capernaum by the Sea of Galilee.**

   Matthew 4:13–17: *And* **leaving Nazareth he went and lived in Capernaum** *by the sea, in the territory of Zebulun and Naphtali, 14 so that what was spoken by the prophet Isaiah might be fulfilled: 15 "The land of Zebulun*

   Synagogue at Capernaum

   and the land of Naphtali, the way of the sea, beyond the Jordan, Galilee of the Gentiles—16 the people dwelling in darkness have seen a great light, and for those dwelling in the region and shadow of death, on them a light has dawned." 17 From that time Jesus began to preach, saying, "Repent, for the kingdom of heaven is at hand."

5. **Jesus was rejected by His own townspeople at Nazareth and was unable to perform many miracles there due to their lack of faith in Him.**

   Luke 4:14–27: *And Jesus returned in the power of the Spirit to Galilee, and a report about him went out through all the surrounding country. 15 And he taught in their synagogues, being glorified by all. 16* **And he came to Nazareth, where he had been brought up**. *And as was his custom, he went to the synagogue on* the Sabbath day, and he stood up to read. 17 And the scroll of the prophet Isaiah was given to him. He unrolled the scroll and found the place where it was written, 18 "The Spirit of the Lord is upon me, because he has anointed me to proclaim good news to the poor. He has sent me to proclaim liberty to the captives and recovering of sight to the blind, to set at liberty those who are

Mount Precipice

oppressed, 19 to proclaim the year of the Lord's favor." 20 And he rolled up the scroll and gave it back to the attendant and sat down. And the eyes of all in the synagogue were fixed on him. 21 And he began to say to them, "Today this Scripture has been fulfilled in your hearing." 22 And all spoke well of him and marveled at the gracious words that were coming from his mouth. And they said, "Is not this Joseph's son?" 23 And he said to them, "Doubtless you will quote to me this proverb, 'Physician, heal yourself.' What we have heard you did at Capernaum, do here in your hometown as well." 24 And he said, "Truly, I say to you, no prophet is acceptable in his hometown. 25 But in truth, I tell you, there were many widows in Israel in the days of Elijah, when the heavens were shut up three years and six months, and a great famine came over all the land, 26 and Elijah was sent to none of them but only to Zarephath, in the land of Sidon, to a woman who was a widow. 27 And there were many lepers in Israel in the time of the prophet Elisha, and none of them was cleansed, but only Naaman the Syrian."

6. **Those who knew Christ best rejected Him and attempted to throw Him off a cliff close to their town. Today, this place is called Mount Precipice.**

   Luke 4:28–30: *When they heard these things, all in the synagogue were filled with wrath. 29 And they rose up and drove him out of the town and brought him to the brow of the hill on which their town was built, so that they could throw him down the cliff. 30 But passing through their midst, he went away.*

Faith Lesson from Nazareth

1. Nazareth had a bad reputation. God oftentimes places light in the dark so the light can illuminate the darkness. Are we being lights where we live?

Mary's Well

2. The people of Nazareth largely rejected Christ. It shouldn't surprise us if we, too, are rejected because of our faith in Christ and adherence to His Word.
3. Christ was rejected, so He understands when we are rejected by our close friends and family members because of our faith in Him.
4. Do we reject Christ by refusing His offer of salvation, by refusing to be obedient to Him, or by not sharing our faith with those around us?

Journal/Notes:

Northern Israel Sites

Nazareth: Church of the Annunciation

Location

1. Nazareth is about 15 miles (24 km.) southwest of the Sea of Galilee and about 23 miles (37 km.) inland from the Mediterranean Sea.
2. The Church of the Annunciation is in the center of the City of Nazareth, on Casa Nova Street.

Historical Background

1. Nazareth had an estimated population of around 300 people during the time of Christ.
2. It was a small farming town where everyone knew each other.
3. Nazareth had a bad reputation.

   John 1:46: *Nathanael said to him, "Can **any good thing** come out of Nazareth?" Philip said to him, "Come and see."*
4. Tradition holds that this home is in the cave grotto in the lower level of the Church of the Annunciation.
5. Christians began venerating the home of Mary and Joseph soon after Christ's death and resurrection. Remains of a Judeo-Christian synagogue at this site show proof of this.
6. In the mid-4th century, Helena, the mother of the Roman Emperor Constantine, commissioned the construction of the Church of the Annunciation based upon tradition and evidence she found at the site. The church was built over the remains of the Judeo-Christian synagogue.
7. The church has been destroyed and rebuilt around 5 times. The Muslims destroyed it in the 7th century. In 1100, the Crusaders arrived and rebuilt the church. In 1620, the Franciscans purchased the ruins and rebuilt them. In 1730, the church was rebuilt again, and in 1877, it was enlarged.

8. From 1955–1969, the church was rebuilt to its current status. It's now a massive two-story church with a modern architectural style. In 1969, when it was completed, it was the largest Christian church in the Middle East.

9. The church has two levels with two separate churches. The upper church level is for Nazareth's Catholic community. The lower level is centered around the grotto, which was the home of Mary and the site of the Annunciation. The remnants of the churches from the second century, Byzantine, and Crusader eras can be seen around the grotto area.

Ruins under the church

10. Another church in Nazareth commemorates the annunciation of the birth of Christ as well. It's the Greek Orthodox Church of the Annunciation, the traditional site held by the Eastern Orthodox churches.

Places of Interest

1. Statue of Mary – Her hands are blackened from touch.
2. Written in Latin across the façade over the triple-doorway entrance is the Bible verse: *"The Word was made flesh and dwelt among us"* (John 1:14).
3. The entryway doors to the church have carvings of significant events that happened in the Old and New Testaments.
4. The current church is a two-story building. The main entrance is on the lower level.
5. On the lower level is the grotto that is believed to be the original home of Mary and the place the angel Gabriel appeared to her.
6. The words written on an altar table at the front of the grotto mean, "Here the Word was made Flesh."
7. On each side of the grotto are the remains of earlier churches.

Northern Israel Sites

8. The upper level of the church serves as the local Roman Catholic parish church.
9. Outside the upper level of the church are excavations and buildings during the time of Christ.
10. Outside the church's lower level is a covered area with mosaic panels of many countries from around the world.

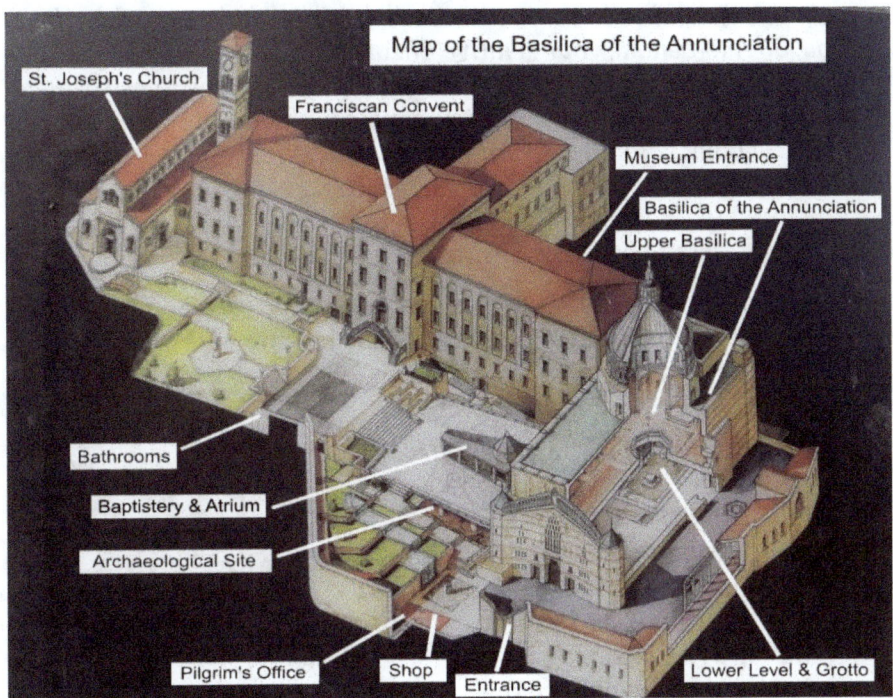

Nazareth in the Bible

1. **Nazareth was the home of Joseph and Mary, and the place where the angel Gabriel was sent to announce to Mary, a virgin, that she would be the mother of Christ the Messiah.**

   Luke 1:26–38: *In the sixth month the angel Gabriel was sent from God to a city of Galilee named **Nazareth**, 27 to a virgin betrothed to a man whose name was Joseph, of the house of David. And the virgin's name was Mary. 28 And he came to her and said, "Greetings, O favored one, the Lord is with you!" 29 But she was greatly troubled at the saying, and tried to discern what sort of greeting this might be. 30 And the angel said to her, "Do not be afraid, Mary, for you have found favor with God. 31 And behold, you will conceive in your* womb and bear a son, and you shall call his name Jesus. 32 He will be great and will be called the Son of the Most High. And the Lord God will give to him the throne of his father David, 33 and he will reign over the house of Jacob forever, and of his kingdom there will be no end." 34 And Mary said to the angel, "How will this be, since I am a virgin?" 35 And the angel answered her, "The Holy Spirit will come upon you, and the power of the Most High will overshadow you; therefore the child to be born will be called holy—the Son of God. 36 And behold, your relative Elizabeth in her old age has also conceived a son, and this is the sixth month with her who was called barren. 37 For nothing will be impossible with God." 38 And Mary said, "Behold, I am the servant of the Lord; let it be to me according to your word." And the angel departed from her.

Faith Lesson from the Life of Mary

1. Mary was a righteous person whom God saw would honor and obey Him with the great gift of being the mother of Christ. Are we devoted to God in such a way that He would entrust to us abundant blessings?

2. Mary did not remain a virgin after giving birth to Christ, as many believe. She had many other children, as we can see all throughout Scripture (Matt. 15:55–56). Are we students of God's Word so we believe the truth, or do we follow what our church or others teach instead? Who is our highest authority in what we believe: people or God's Word?

Church of the Annunciation

3. Mary is not to be worshiped like some do but is an example to us of a person of deep faith and obedience. Do we revere and honor Mary, or do we worship her?

Journal/Notes:

Northern Israel Sites

Sepphoris (Tsipori, Zippori)

Location

1. Sepphoris is located about 4 miles (6 km.) northwest of Nazareth, about 14 miles (23 km.) from the Mediterranean Sea, and about 15 miles (25 km.) from the Sea of Galilee.
2. Because of its close proximity to Nazareth, it was easily accessible by Jesus and His earthly father, Joseph.

Historical Background

1. The city started to grow during the 2nd century BC under Greek rule.
2. Later, under Roman rule during the time of Christ, Herod Antipas (the son of Herod the Great) invested in it significantly and made it "the ornament of Galilee." It was a sophisticated Roman city with all the luxuries of modern life at that time. It included a network of colonnaded paved streets, markets, residential houses, public buildings, bathhouses, a theater, and a synagogue.
3. Sepphoris rose to recognized status during the century before Christ because it was located right on one of the main trade routes linking Africa with Europe and Asia called "The Via Maris" (way of the sea). Therefore, it was a wealthy city.
4. It was also a military city guarded well by Roman troops.
5. Sepphoris was the capital of the Galilee area during the time of Christ.
6. In order to rebuild the city, Herod Antipas used a massive workforce.
7. Because Nazareth was so close to Sepphoris, and because Jesus was a Tekton (Greek for a construction worker of various types), Jesus and His father undoubtedly worked here.
8. So, in part, it's also where Jesus grew in wisdom and stature and in

favor with God and man (Luke 2:52).

9. Because it was mainly a Jewish city, it was given its Hebrew name, Zippori, because it sits on a hilltop like a bird (Zippor).
10. Sepphoris is also known as the Mosaic City, as some of the best mosaics in all of Israel are found here. More than 40 mosaic floors reveal the bustling life of a Roman city and the luxury it afforded.
11. After Herod's death in 4 BC, the Roman army rose up and halted a rebellion of Jewish rebels led by a man named Judas. Many of these rebels, numbering several thousand, were killed. However, according to Josephus, 2,000 of them were kept alive to be crucified on its streets and nearby roads in the area. These mass crucifixions were carried out to instill fear in others who might consider rebelling against Roman rule.

12. Sepphoris did not join the Jewish rebellion in 66-70 AD and was therefore spared destruction.
13. After the destruction of Jerusalem in 70 AD, Sepphoris became a center of Jewish learning and seat of the Sanhedrin supreme court. The Mishnah, the first authoritative collection of Jewish Oral Law, was compiled here.
14. Sepphoris witnessed Byzantine, Crusader, and Ottoman rule in the centuries following.

Places of Interest

1. Park Entrance
2. Water System
3. Decumanus Street
4. Nile House & Mosaics
5. Cardo

6. Public Building
7. Dionysus (god of wine) Building & Mosaics
8. Fortress
9. Residential Area
10. Theater
11. Synagogue

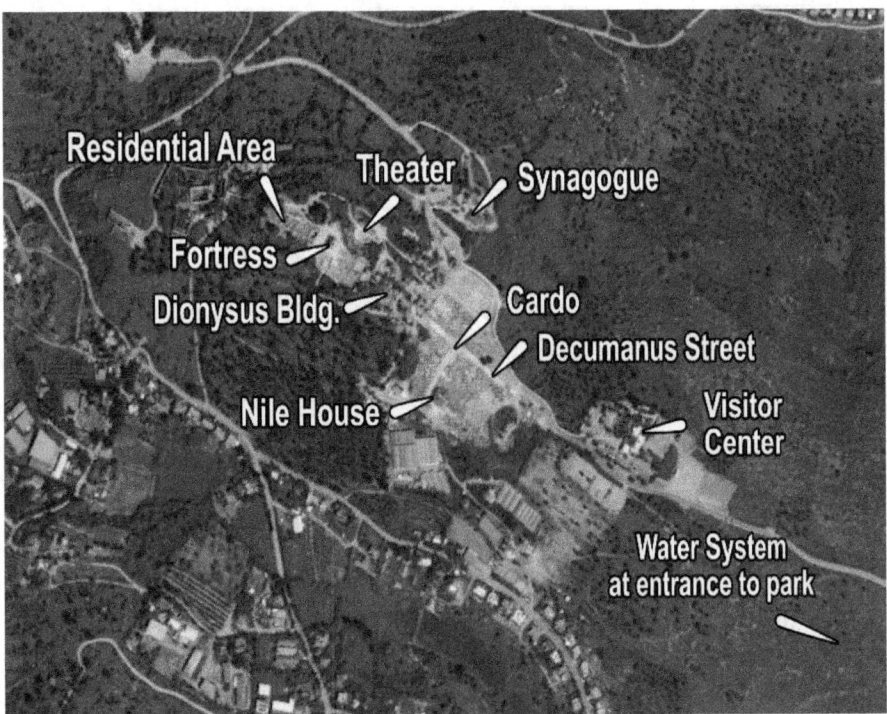

Sepphoris in the Bible

While Sepphoris is not mentioned in the Bible, it is significant for several reasons:

1. **It was nearby to Nazareth and employed many carpenters. Because Jesus was a construction worker, it's very likely Jesus worked here before starting His earthly ministry.**
2. **After the death of Jesus' earthly father, Joseph, Christ became the chief financial provider for His family. Christ was very responsible in caring for His family and expects us to do the same.**

   2 Thessalonians 3:10–11: *For even when we were with you, we*

would give you this command: If anyone is not willing to work, let him not eat. 11 For we hear that some among you walk in idleness, not busy at work, but busybodies.

John 19:26–27: *When Jesus saw his mother and the disciple whom he loved standing nearby, he said to his mother, "Woman, behold, your son!" 27 Then he said to the disciple, "Behold, your mother!" And from that hour the disciple took her to his own home.*

3. **It appears Jesus used references about this city in His teachings.**

   Matthew 5:14: *You are the light of the world. A city set on a hill cannot be hidden. Nor do people light a lamp and put it under a basket, but on a stand, and it gives light to all in the house.*

   Sepphoris was certainly a city on a hill. In fact, that's what the name of this city means.

   Fortress

   Matthew 6:2–4: *Thus, when you give to the needy, sound no trumpet before you, as the hypocrites do in the synagogues and in the streets, that they may be praised by others. Truly, I say to you; they have received their reward. 3 But when you give to the needy, do not let your left hand know what your right hand is doing, 4 so that your giving may be in secret. And your Father who sees in secret will reward you.*

   - The word for actor in Greek is "hypocrite." Because these actors would walk the streets sounding their horns to advertise an upcoming event at the city theater, Jesus used them as an example of what not to do when giving to others and serving God.

4. **Jesus likely used the example of the mass crucifixion carried out by the Romans against the Jewish revolt here to teach about the cost of being His disciple.**

Mark 8:34–38: *And calling the crowd to him with his disciples, he said to them, "If anyone would come after me, let him deny himself and take up his cross and follow me. 35 For whoever would save his life will lose it, but whoever loses his life for my sake and the gospel's will save it. 36 For what does it profit a man to gain the whole world and forfeit his soul? 37 For what can a man give in return for his soul? 38 For whoever is ashamed of me and of my words in this adulterous and sinful generation, of him will the Son of Man also be ashamed when he comes in the glory of his Father with the holy angels."*

- Christ taught about the cost of following him in several places during His ministry. In this account in Mark, He was teaching in the upper Galilee area at Caesarea Philippi, which is not far from Sepphoris.

Cardo showing chariot grooves

- It's very likely Christ's audience would have personally witnessed the crucifixions here in Sepphoris or seen others.

- To the Jewish mind, Christ's teaching would have sent a powerful and sober message of what Christ was asking of His followers. He was calling for total commitment, even commitment to death.

- Christ also used the imagery of crucifixion to teach us how we should daily crucify our personal desires that are contrary to God's desires.

- Sepphoris was certainly an adulterous and sinful city that Christ probably referred to in Mark 8:38.

Faith Lesson from Sepphoris

1. Jesus was a hard worker. Are we hard workers as well?
2. Jesus provided for His family after the death of His father. He also took care of His mother's future needs as He was being crucified. Do we provide and take care of our family members?
3. Jesus was undoubtedly good at what He did as a construction worker. Do we develop our skills to be good at what we do as well?
4. We should emulate Jesus in not only His spiritual side but also in His work ethic, work skills, and family responsibilities.

Crusader Fortress

5. Jesus grew in wisdom and stature and in favor with God and man prior to His earthly ministry. Are we doing the same?
6. Jesus likely used Sepphoris as an example of how we should be lights on a hill. Are we letting our lights shine brightly, or are we dim lights to those who know and see us?
7. Jesus likely used the actors in Sepphoris who blew their loud trumpets as an example of what we should not do when we give and serve God. Do we serve for God's glory alone, or do we serve for the praise and esteem of others?

Journal/Notes:

Other Sites in Northern Israel

Acre (Akko, Acco, Ptolemais)

Located about 9 miles (14 km.) north of Haifa, Acre was one of the best seaports in Israel.

Acre was allotted to the tribe of Asher, but they were never able to conquer it (Josh. 19:24–31; Judg. 1:31).

It was similar to Tyre and Sidon, cities the Israelites failed to conquer. As a result, Acre became a fortress city of unusual strength that stood up against its many attackers.

However, when Assyria arose to power, Acre was conquered and came under its control. When Assyria fell from world power, Acre, along with other Phoenician towns, came under the rule of Babylon, and then later, to Persia.

Modern Acre with seaport

In the Seleucid period (BC 312–65), Acre rose to prominence in the battles between the Seleucids and the Ptolemies. The Ptolemies had control of it during the struggles after the death of Alexander the Great and made it their stronghold on the coast. At this time, the city of Acre was changed to the name Ptolemais. This would be the name it would be known as during the Greek and Roman occupations of Israel. Therefore, the New Testament authors refer to Acre as Ptolemais (Acts 21:7).

In the period of the Crusaders, Acre was the most famous stronghold on the coast.

It declined after the Crusader period and fell into the hands of the Ottomans under Selim I in 1516.

Belvoir Fortress

This Crusader castle is located on a hill of the Naphtali Plateau, 12 miles (20 km.) south of the Sea of Galilee.

This impressive structure sits about 1,641 ft. (500 m.) above the Jordan Valley, which was a strategic location during the time of the Crusades. Designed to withstand the Muslim invaders, the fortress provided strong combat positioning as well as an amazing view of the surrounding area.

Belvoir Fortress

Built in 1168 by the Hospitallers order, it withstood a year and a half siege by Saladin's forces. The structure itself consists of an outer and an inner square fortress. It is still well-preserved, and visitors can explore the grounds while taking in a stunning view of the Jordan Valley, the Sea of Galilee, and the Golan Heights. It's the most complete and preserved Crusader fortress in Israel.

Tel Jezreel (Yizreel)

Jezreel, located in the fertile Jezreel Valley, is about 24 miles (38 km.) east of the Mediterranean Sea and about 17 miles (28 km.) southwest of the Sea of Galilee.

Tel Jezreel

Jezreel was a major biblical city, and during the 9th century BC, it was the northern capital of the Israelite Kingdom.

Northern Israel Sites

When Saul and Jonathan were killed in battle on Mount Gilboa, news of this event came from Jezreel. Mephibosheth, Jonathan's son, became crippled when his nurse fell while carrying him as she ran in haste after hearing the terrible news of Jonathan's death (2 Sam. 4:4).

After the Kingdom of Israel was divided in around 930 BC, King Ahab made Jezreel one of his royal residences, erecting a palace here (1 Kings 21:1).

At Jezreel lived King Ahab's wife, who instituted the worship to the false gods of Baal and Asherah. This provoked God to send a drought that lasted 3 years. It ended with the great showdown between Elijah and the 850 false prophets of Baal and Asherah. God sent fire from heaven that consumed Elijah's altar to show the nation of Israel He was God. Afterward, Elijah killed all the false prophets (1 Kings 18).

The vineyard of Naboth was by King Ahab's palace in Jezreel. Ahab wanted the vineyard for a vegetable garden, but Naboth refused to sell it. So Ahab's wicked wife, Jezebel, arranged for Naboth to be wrongly accused and executed so Ahab could rob his land (1 Kings 21).

Apparently, it was on the city's eastern wall from which Jehu entered when he ordered Jezebel (King Ahab's wife) to be thrown down according to prophecy. Some of her blood spattered on the wall when she landed, and the dogs ate her body (2 Kings 9:30–37).

Nimrod Fortress National Park

Nimrod Fortress is situated in the northernmost part of Israel, just a few miles north of Caesarea Philippi. It's on a ridge rising some 2,600 ft. (800 m.) above sea level and is the biggest Crusader castle in Israel. The mountain-top stronghold overlooks the deep narrow valley separating Mount Hermon from the Golan Heights and the road linking the Galilee with Damascus (present-day Syria).

Nimrod Fortress

The Crusaders built it in the Middle Ages to guard this major access route against armies coming from the west. On the eastern edge of the fortress was a large keep (a keep is a fortress within a fortress), protected by large rectangular towers. In the west, it was separated from the main fortress by a moat, accessed by a bridge. The keep served as living quarters for the commander of the fortress. In times of siege, it became an additional defense position. The fortress is named after a biblical hero, the hunter, Nimrod, the great warrior (Gen. 10:8-9) who, according to local tradition, dwelt on this summit.

Timeline of Israel

Why it's so important to understand a brief overview of the historical periods of Israel.

The Holy Land is an old place, about the oldest in the world! While in the Holy Land, you'll be seeing things as old as 6,000 years. That's old! Different periods of history will be referred to when describing Israel's holy sites and places. Please realize that there will likely be several key events at a particular site that have taken place there. Each event will have happened during a specific period in Israel's history. If you can understand the different periods a little, you'll get much more out of your experience.

Chronology of Time Used by Archaeologist and Historians
- Early Bronze Age   4000–2000 BC
- Middle Bronze Age   2000–1500 BC
- Late Bronze Age   1500–1200 BC
- Iron 1 Age   1200–1000 BC
- Iron 2 Age   1000–586 BC

Canaanite Period   4000–1875 BC
- 4000 BC – Canaanites inhabit the land of Israel.
- 2500 BC – Noah and the Great Flood.
- 2100 BC – Tower of Babel
- 2095 BC – Abraham moves to the land of Canaan from Ur of the Chaldeans.
- 1880 BC – Jacob and his family move to Egypt to live with Joseph.

Israelite Period   1450–965 BC
- 1450 BC – Exodus of the Israelites from Egypt.
- 1406 BC – Jews enter the Promised Land.
- 1012 BC – Saul unifies the 12 Hebrew tribes into the United Kingdom of Israel.
- 1010–970 BC – David's reign.

First Temple Period   970–586 BC
- 970–925 BC – Solomon's reign; glory years of the Kingdom of Israel.
- 950 BC – Solomon builds the magnificent temple on Mount

Timeline of Israel

Moriah in Jerusalem (same place Abraham intended to sacrifice Isaac).

- 926 BC – Kingdom of Israel divides because of Solomon's sins. Jeroboam reigns over the northern Kingdom of Israel from Samaria. Rehoboam reigns over the southern Kingdom of Israel from Jerusalem.
- 722 BC – Assyrians conquer and deport most of the northern Kingdom of Israel to Assyria.
- 586 BC – Babylonians conquer Jerusalem and Judah under Nebuchadnezzar and deport most of the southern Kingdom of Judah to Babylon.

Second Temple Period   535–444 BC

- 535 BC – Many Jews return from Babylonia; Second Temple began to be rebuilt.
- 458 BC – Ezra returns to Jerusalem with second wave of Jews to continue rebuilding the Second Temple.
- 444 BC – Nehemiah returns to Jerusalem to rebuild the city walls.

Hellenistic Period (Greek Rule)   333–167 BC

- 333 BC – Alexander the Great defeats the Persian Empire and sets out to conquer the world. After his sudden death in 323 BC, the Greek Empire is divided. During this period the Bible is translated into Greek (the Septuagint).

Hasmonean Period (Maccabean Rule)   167–63 BC

- 167 BC – When the Jews were prohibited from practicing Judaism, and their temple was desecrated as part of an effort to impose Greek-oriented culture and customs on the entire population, the Jews revolted. First led by Mattathias of the priestly Hasmonean family and then by his son Judah the Maccabee, the Jews subsequently entered Jerusalem and purified the temple. This purification of the temple is remembered by the Jewish Holiday, Hanukkah (164 BC).

Roman Period (Roman Rule)   63 BC–330 AD

- 63 BC – Jerusalem is captured by Roman general Pompey.
- 37 BC–4 BC – Herod, Roman vassal king, rules the Land of Israel. He enlarges the Temple Mount and rebuilds the temple. He also

builds other monumental projects, including Caesarea, Herodian, Cave of the Patriarchs, and Masada.

- 4 BC – Jesus is born in Bethlehem.
- 27–30 AD – Ministry of Jesus.
- 30 AD – Jesus crucified.
- 66 AD – Jewish revolt against the Romans.
- 70 AD – Destruction of Jerusalem and Second Temple.
- 74 AD – Fall of Masada.
- 132 AD – Bar Kokhba Revolt. Roman Emperor Hadrian destroys Jerusalem and builds Aelia Capitolina, a pagan city in its place. Many holy sites are preserved, but with pagan shrines on them.

Byzantine Period (Eastern Roman Empire Rule)   330–614 AD

- 313 – Emperor Constantine recognizes Christianity, later becoming a Christian himself.
- 326 – Constantine's mother, Helena, goes to the Holy Land and builds many churches and basilicas on holy sites.

Persian Period   614–628 AD

- 614 – Persian conquest of the Holy Land. Many churches and monasteries destroyed.

Byzantine Period Reestablished   628–638 AD

- 628 – Holy Land recaptured by the Byzantines.

Muslim/Arab Period   638–1099 AD

- 638 – Muslim/Arab conquest of the Holy Land completed. Rule is by Caliphs from Damascus, then from Baghdad, and then Egypt.
- 691 – On top of the First and Second Temples in Jerusalem, the Dome of the Rock is built by Caliph Abd el-Malik.

Crusader Period   1099–1291 AD

- 1099 – Crusaders (Catholic armies from Rome) conquer Jerusalem and many parts of Israel.
- 1147 – Second Crusade arrives in the Holy Land.
- 1187 – Destruction of the Crusader army by Muslim leader Saladin. Collapse of Crusader Kingdom begins.

Timeline of Israel

- 1265 – Mamelukes, led by Sultan Beybars, conquer the Holy Land.
- 1270 – Final Crusade arrives, and all its participants massacred.
- 1291 – Last Crusader stronghold of Acco taken, ending Crusader rule.

Mamluk (Muslim) Period   1291–1517 AD

- 1291 – Mamluk rule begins.
- 1333 – Franciscan Order established in Jerusalem. Its members care for holy places and pilgrims.
- By the end of the Middle Ages, the country's urban centers were virtually in ruins, most of Jerusalem was abandoned, and the small Jewish community was poverty-stricken. The period of Mamluk decline was darkened by political and economic upheavals, plagues, locust invasions, and devastating earthquakes.

Ottoman (Muslim) Period   1517–1917 AD

- 1517 – Following the Ottoman conquest in 1517, the land was divided into four districts and attached administratively to the province of Damascus and ruled from Istanbul.
- 1520 – Suleiman the Magnificent rebuilds the city walls of Jerusalem.
- 1799 – Napoleon Bonaparte invades Israel but fails to capture it and is forced to leave.
- 1860 – The first neighborhood, Mishkenot Sha'ananim, is built outside of Jerusalem's city walls.
- 1882 – First large-scale immigration to Israel, mainly from Russia.
- 1904 – Second large-scale immigration from Russia and Poland.

British Period   1917–1948 AD

- 1917 – British Foreign Minister Lord Balfour issued on November 2, 1917, the so-called Balfour Declaration, which gave official support for the "establishment in Israel of a national home for the Jewish people" with the commitment not to be prejudiced against the rights of the non-Jewish communities.
- 1947 – The United Nations approved the partition of Israel into separate Jewish and Arab states on November 29, 1947.

State of Israel Period   1948 to Present

- 1948 – On the day when the British Mandate in Palestine expired, the State of Israel was instituted on May 14, 1948, by the Jewish National Council under the presidency of David Ben Gurion.
- 1948–1949 – The Arab-Israeli War; the Arabs refused to accept the newly established State of Israel. Egypt, Syria, Transjordan, Lebanon, and Iraq attack Israel, but within a year, Israel defeated its attackers.
- 1950 – Western Jerusalem was proclaimed the capital city of Israel on January 23, 1950.
- 1956 – The Suez Crisis: Israelis invade Egyptian territory in October of 1956.
- 1956 – After Egyptian President Gamal Abdel Nasser nationalized the company which administered the Suez Canal, a joint attack by the French and British was launched. Egypt suffered military disaster on November 2, 1956. Israel captured the Sinai Peninsula, but after international condemnation, Israel was forced to withdraw.
- 1967 – Six-Day War: after Egypt closed the Straits of Tiran on May 22, 1967, Israel launched an attack on Egyptian, Jordanian, Syrian, and Iraqi airports on June 5, 1967. After six days, Israel conquered Jerusalem, the Golan Heights, Sinai, and the West Bank.
- 1973 – Yom Kippur War: on October 6, 1973, on the Jewish holiday of Yom Kippur, Syria and Egypt launched a surprise attack against Israel. After initial success of the attackers, Israel managed to cross the Suez into Egypt and endangered Cairo. After the intervention of the USA and USSR, military operations ended on October 25, 1973.
- 1978 – The Camp David Accord was signed by Israeli Prime Minister Menahen Begin, and Egyptian President Anvar as Sadat in September 1978, in Camp David, USA. Israel agreed to withdraw from the occupied Sinai Peninsula.
- 1979 – The Israel-Egypt Peace Treaty was signed on March 26, 1979, in Washington.

Maps of Israel

Sea of Galilee & Northern Biblical Sites Guide

Twelve Tribes of Israel

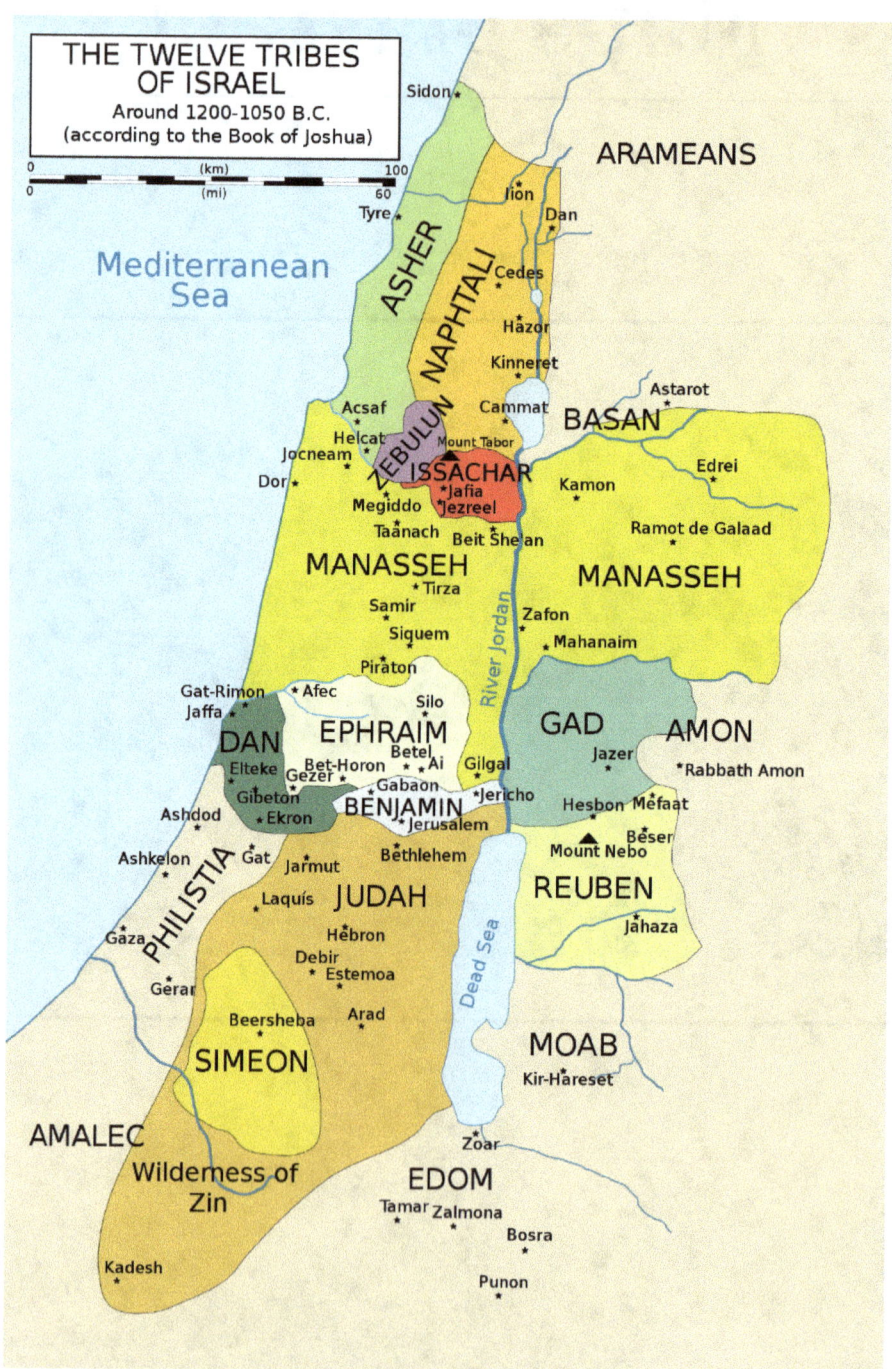

Divided Kingdom

Regions of Israel

Maps of Israel

Israel Today

Travel Orientation

Travel Orientation

Understanding the Holy Sites in Israel

The Need to Understand What You're Going to See

It would be wonderful if the Holy Land was exactly the same as it was 2,000 years ago when Christ walked its paths, or 4,000 years ago when Abraham traversed its hillsides and valleys. However, 4,000 years is a long time, and there have been many changes that have taken place during this time span. It's hard for us to understand, but 4,000 or even 2,000 years is a long time! Because of its strategic location in the world, no other country has had as many kingdoms occupy it or as many battles fought on its soil as Israel. This, along with time, has led to much change to Israel and its holy sites.

The good news is that many of the biblical sites are in their natural state and appear much the same as they did when the events that happened there occurred. Other sites have had monuments, churches, or basilicas built near, or on them, and are not exactly as they appeared when the events that occurred there happened. Also, many sites have had many events happen in one spot over thousands of years, so it would be impossible to have each event preserved just the way it happened.

Understanding What Some of The Holy Sites Will Be Like

Many of these monuments, churches, or basilicas will have a Catholic, Arabic, or Mid-Eastern look. They're very different from what we're accustomed to seeing, and at first glance, you might find this unattractive. You also might disagree with the religious backgrounds of some of these sites and feel somewhat uncomfortable as well. In addition, you most likely will find other people visiting the Holy Land from other countries who are actually worshiping and kissing some of the adornments on these sites. On a previous trip to Israel, some in our group found all this a little repulsive and chose not to enter some of these holy sites. Because of these possible negative reactions, we would like to provide you with a little background and history about how these holy sites have been preserved so your sightseeing experience can be the best as possible during your time in the Holy Land.

Sea of Galilee & Northern Biblical Sites Guide

A Little History

Even before the time of Christ and afterward, many of the holy sites were marked out and preserved. Then, about 300 years after the time of Christ, the Roman Empire (world power at that time) embraced Christianity. At that time, the mother of Emperor Constantine (Helena) was one of the first of the royal family to convert to Christianity. Later, Emperor Constantine did as well. Helena came to the Holy Land and wanted to preserve some of the holy sites, so she had churches, monuments, and basilicas built over some of the key holy places. These included the Church of the Holy Sepulture, Church of the Nativity, Basilica in the Garden of Gethsemane, Church of the Annunciation, and others. Helena, and others throughout history, felt such emotion and awe at these holy sites that they wanted to honor and preserve them for future generations. The Early Church during this period was the first to be in charge of these sites, and then because the Early Church slowly evolved into what we know as the Catholic Church, many of these holy sites came under the care of the Catholic Church. The monuments, churches, and basilicas were not always Catholic in nature, so we shouldn't assume that they shared the same religious views at their inception.

There were others as well that came to the Holy Land to build churches, monuments, and basilicas on these holy sites (Eastern Orthodox Church, Armenians, Russians, Greeks, etc.). Their hearts felt the same awe and emotion as others who came, so they too built on or by these holy sites to honor and preserve them.

Some of these holy sites are ancient (from as old as 5,000 years), and the churches have a Mid-Eastern style look.

Gratefulness to Those Who Preserved the Biblical Sites

If it hadn't been for those who built monuments or churches on or by the holy sites, they would have had other buildings, roads, and infrastructure built over them and lost to the world forever. These early pilgrims felt the same awe and emotion you will feel, and we certainly can't fault them for this.

Because of all the adornments and construction over the centuries, it's hard to imagine how some of these sites would have looked in their original setting. However, the years of activity and tradition at these holy sites give greater weight to their authenticity. And while we might disagree with the decorations, atmosphere of these places, and religious backgrounds, we can certainly appreciate and admire all the devotion and sacrifice made to preserve them.

Some Might Find These Churches, Monuments, and Basilicas Repulsive

Part of the reason some might find the places they see in Israel as repulsive will have to do with a difference in religious faith. Another reason is due to a misunderstanding of style. These holy sites have a very different style than what we're accustomed to in modern churches. Most of the oldest churches we see today in our own countries are just a few hundred years old and have somewhat the same architecture and style from our modern era. As a result, we're just not used to seeing churches close to 1,500 years old, and older.

Closing Thoughts

1. Entering these churches, monuments, and basilicas to see these holy sites doesn't mean we're in any way embracing and accepting their religious beliefs.

2. While the style, religious background, and adornments might not be to our taste, the motives of those who preserved these sites seem to be noble and honorable. As you see these sites, you will understand why these early pilgrims wanted to preserve them.

3. It's important to note that we, from a modern mindset, have a different view and taste regarding building styles. Because to us, something 200-400 years old seems really ancient, we need to realize that seeing something 1,500 years old has an entirely different architectural look and sense to it than what we're accustomed to seeing.

Hopefully, this info will help you. As mentioned, on a previous trip to Israel, some didn't really understand these things beforehand, and it took them a bit to get themselves wrapped around some of these concepts. It was kind of a self-discovery process. For this reason, this orientation and background are provided so you can get the most out of your Holy Land Experience and not get bogged down in this area.

How to Get the Most Out of Your Holy Land Trip

How to See What Many Don't See in the Holy Land

Understand that half of what there is to see in the Holy Land is hidden from most that walk her paths. They are unseen spiritual truths, only revealed to the sensitive and spiritual of heart. Try to get as close to God as you can prior, and during your time in the Holy Land, so you can see and hear things that many don't see during their visit there. The Holy Land is not just places and historical artifacts; it's an experience — an experience that is spiritual in nature and eye-opening for those who can see in this realm.

You Won't Be Able to See Everything

It would be great to see every detail at every holy site, but that would take months, if not years, to do. It's important to understand that there is a lot to see and, therefore, just the highlights can be seen. You'll be eating the frosting off the cake and won't be able to eat the whole thing. As a result, please don't be discouraged if you can't spend as much time in each place as you'd wish. You'll have to move along to see just the highlights, and if you stay too long at one place, that means you'll be saying "No" to another.

Your Trip Won't be Perfect

It would be wonderful if you could be guaranteed a perfect trip with a perfect experience, but that's just not reality. Going to the Holy Land is undoubtedly the closest you'll get to the "Trip of a Lifetime," but please don't get your hopes up so high that you're let down and feel discouraged if it doesn't turn out as you dreamed. Your trip won't be perfect. Your leader and the rest in your group will probably not live up to your expectations either. The only perfect person on the trip will be you (well, maybe not exactly perfect, but pretty close to it, lol). So just prepare yourself to understand that things just aren't going to be flawless.

Trust God for Your Experience

It's also easy to have preconceived ideas of what to expect; the emotions you're going to feel, the dreams you might have of the Holy Land, and the experience you want to have. Please try to set some of

Travel Orientation

these aside and trust God to give you the experience He has for you. Don't get everything built up so high that it would be impossible to fulfill them. Trust God to bless you and teach you what He has for you. He's the One who's worked everything out for you to go, and I'm certain He has special things to teach you. Trust in Him and be looking for what He has for you. And after everything is said and done, be content with what He gives you.

Understanding Group Travel Dynamics

Traveling with Others

Part of the joy and richness of your Holy Land Experience will come from sharing it with others. Going somewhere alone is never as much fun as doing it with someone else. The impact and fullness of the experience will come alive as it's experienced as a group rather than as an individual or couple. For this reason, you'll want to consider a few things to make your Holy Land Experience the best as possible.

Try to Think as a Group and Not as an Individual

Traveling as a group is very different from traveling as an individual or couple. There will be other team members in your group, and each person needs to realize they're part of a larger event than just themselves. The whole team will be depending on others to be punctual, courteous, thoughtful, and pleasant. Try to take into consideration that what you do affects everyone else on the team.

Try to Keep Up with the Group

It will be important that you keep up with the group and not linger too long seeing things during your travels. Each day it is wise to appoint a "Follow-up Person" who'll bring up the group's rear and make sure everyone stays together. Because you'll be seeing some really interesting things, it will be easy to get lost in these and forget that there are other things to see as well.

Try to Be Punctual

Everything from wake-up times, mealtimes, arrival times, departure times, and the site-seeing schedule for each day needs to be considered. Because you are spending a lot of money and taking precious time out of your busy life to experience the Holy Land, you'll want to be as punctual as possible so you and your team can see everything as planned. Your group can only be as fast as the slowest person, so try to be punctual and thoughtful of others. If you tend to be a late person, consider getting a head start on things by starting earlier than normal so you can be on time.

Travel Orientation

Try to Be Patient and Courteous

Be aware that sometime during the trip, you'll likely feel tired, a bit irritated with others, or upset at something that's happened. Do your best to overlook the faults of others and try to keep yourself in check. Also, realize that we have an enemy who will do his best to take away from our experience by using others or problems. Be alert and prayerful! Keep yourself close to God and do your best to love others and take everything in stride.

Try to Be Rested Up Before Your Holy Land Trip

Because you're going to be expending a lot of energy during the trip, try to get as rested as possible before departure. To illustrate this point, we'll use the term "gauges" to help us out. We all know that most of our vehicles have gauges: gas gauge, temperature gauge, oil gauge, etc. Using this analogy for our bodies, we all have bodily gauges as well. We have physical, emotional, mental, and spiritual gauges. Before your trip, try to get your bodily gauges as full as possible. By doing so, you'll get more out of your trip and be more joyful and patient with others.

Tips for filling up your bodily gauges before trip departure:

- Try and scale down on your activities and output before the trip. For example, cut back on meetings, outings, get-togethers, and social events.
- Get plenty of sleep.
- Get plenty of exercise (you'll be doing quite a bit of walking, so try to get in walking shape before the trip).
- Get as much of your responsibilities and commitments done ahead of time, and don't wait until the last minute to take care of things. There will be plenty of last-minute things to do, so don't add to them by procrastinating.
- Try to get packed and ready at your earliest convenience. If you need to shop for trip items, try to do so plenty of time in advance.

By taking into consideration these tips, you'll start your trip with your bodily gauges full and not empty. And when you think about it, who would start a long journey with their car having an empty gas tank and little or no oil in the engine?

Sea of Galilee & Northern Biblical Sites Guide

Travel Tips for Israel

1. Get in shape physically before you go to Israel. You will be doing a lot of walking, so the better shape you're in, the easier and more pleasant your time will be. At least a month before your trip, start walking at least 15-30 minutes a day.
2. Activate your credit/debit cards before departure to Israel.
3. Make sure your Passport is up to date and valid. It must have at least 6 months before expiration from your last day in Israel to be valid.
4. Don't shave your body before taking a dip in the Dead Sea. The salt and minerals will irritate your skin.
5. Don't show public affection with the opposite sex, especially on the Temple Mount and Muslim sites.
6. Don't be afraid to bargain for purchases at marketplaces. It's expected, so take part in it.
7. Establish meeting places at each site so that if for some reason you get lost or separated, you can find each other.
8. Carry a water bottle and stay hydrated.
9. Pack layered types of clothing instead of heavy clothes.
10. Carry your personal items in a safe place on your person.
11. Take a good camera or video camera.
12. Get used to people smoking as it's very common in Israel and the Middle East.
13. Many Israelis are not religious but secular. This might seem strange, but it's true.
14. Carry a copy of your Passport.
15. Women should dress very modestly, especially when visiting holy sites.
16. Men should wear hats when visiting Jewish holy sites.
17. Men should not wear hats when visiting Christian holy sites.

Travel Orientation

Packing List

Clothes

Dressing in layers is best when considering your clothes. For the most part, the weather will be warm and sunny during the summer and cooler in the winter. Following are some suggested items that might be helpful:

- Casual pants for hiking and sightseeing (casual can be worn the whole trip).
- Nicer shorts are okay at many places. However, at some sites like the Temple Mount, Western Wall, etc., pants are recommended. Also, for women, being very modest is recommended at these sites as well.
- Casual long sleeve shirts
- Short sleeve shirts
- Bathing suit (for the Dead Sea if you want to take a dip)
- 2 Plastic bags for wet clothes.
- Undergarments
- Socks
- Light jacket
- Sturdy walking shoes with traction for many stone paths and roads you'll traverse. FYI- many of the streets are paved with stone, and it's challenging to wear shoes with awkward heels/soles on uneven pavement.
- Sleepwear
- Hat for sun protection purposes.
- Men will need to wear a hat or equivalent on their heads when entering Jewish sites and synagogues.
- Ladies will need a shawl or equivalent when entering Muslim areas.

General Items

- Slimline travel Bible
- Small notebook and pen for taking notes
- Travel alarm
- Flashlight (mini) or cell phone with flashlight

- Camera/video camera
- Film or storage disks for your camera (bring plenty, because they're much more expensive in Israel)
- Daypack/backpack (can be used as an airplane carry-on and for travel in Israel).
- Ziplock bags for lunches and for putting the relics in you might gather along the way in Israel.
- Umbrella – small contractible type
- Sunglasses
- Plug adapter for plugging devices into the outlets in Israel.

  Note: The outlets in Israel are different than the states. You'll need this adapter for plugging things in to be charged, etc.
- Charger converter needed for Israel (needed for charging cameras, etc.) Note: Electricity in Israel is 220 volts. In America, and many other countries, it's 110 volts. Many electronic devices today can adapt to both voltages. However, if you plan to take an item that cannot use 220 volts, you will need a converter.

Personal Items
- Toothbrush
- Toothpaste
- Deodorant
- Lip balm
- Razor
- After-shave
- Band-Aids
- Feminine items
- Sunscreen
- Tylenol/Ibuprofen
- Eyeglasses/contact lenses
- Prescription medicines

Travel Orientation

Documents & Items to Carry with You at all Times

There are several options for carrying your money and important documents with you on your trip. For example, you can use a money belt (waist style or necklace style) or pockets on your pants or shirt that can be buttoned and are secure.

- Passport – Must have 6 months left before expiring from the dates of your trip.
- Copy of your Passport
- Driver's License
- Cash
- Credit/Debit Card (make sure to activate your cards for Israel or international travel).

    Note: It's handy to use your debit card for drawing out Shekels for spending money in Israel. You'll also get the best exchange rate by using it as well.

- Travel Visa received in Israel at customs.

    Special Note: When arriving in Israel, you'll go through customs to receive your visa for your stay in Israel. It will be a small piece of paper. ***Please don't lose it!*** You will need it on several occasions while in the country. You can tuck it away in your Passport if you'd like.

About the Author

Todd M. Fink is the founder and director of Go Missions to Mexico and Holy Land Site Ministries. He holds the following degrees: Bachelor of Theology from Freelandia Bible College, Master of Divinity studies at Western Seminary, Master of Theology from Freedom Bible College and Seminary, Master of Divinity from Trinity Theological Seminary, and a Ph.D. in theology from Trinity Theological Seminary.

He served as youth/associate pastor for 11 years at an Evangelical church in Oregon (1987–1998).

Todd is currently serving as pastor and missionary with Go Missions to Mexico Ministries in Mexico (1998–present).

He also is serving with Holy Land Site ministries and has a passion for the Holy Land. He has developed a large website and YouTube channel with videos and teachings about almost every site in Israel. In addition, he leads tour trips to Israel and has written books about the Holy Land.

Todd is an author, speaker, and teacher. He has a deep passion for God's Word and enjoys helping people understand its eternal truths.

He is married to his lovely wife, Letsy, and has four grown children.

Books by Todd M. Fink

Israel Biblical Sites Travel Guide

Israel Biblical Sites Bible Companion

Jerusalem & Central Israel Biblical Sites Guide

Sea of Galilee & Northern Israel Biblical Sites Guide

Negev & Southern Israel Biblical Sites Guide

Biblical Discipleship: Essential Components for Reaching Spiritual Maturity

Biblical Discipleship: Essential Components for Reaching Spiritual Maturity 16 Week Study Guide

What is the Gospel and How to Share It

Discovering the True Riches of Life

A Biblical Analysis of Corrective Church Discipline

Discipulado Bíblico

Discipulado Bíblico Guía de Estudio

Please visit: ToddMichaelFink.com to see or purchase books.

Connect with Todd

Email: holylandsite.com@gmail.com

Facebook: Todd Mike Fink

Facebook Ministry Page: Holy Land Site

YouTube Channel: Holy Land Site

Websites:

HolyLandSite.com

ToddMichaelFink.com

SelahBookPress.com

GoMissionsToMexico.com

MinisteriosCasaDeLuz.com